Blood: A Very Short Introduction

VERY SHORT INTRODUCTIONS are for anyone wanting a stimulating and accessible way into a new subject. They are written by experts, and have been translated into more than 40 different languages.

The series began in 1995, and now covers a wide variety of topics in every discipline. The VSI library now contains over 450 volumes—a Very Short Introduction to everything from Psychology and Philosophy of Science to American History and Relativity—and continues to grow in every subject area.

Very Short Introductions available now:

ACCOUNTING Christopher Nobes
ADOLESCENCE Peter K. Smith
ADVERTISING Winston Fletcher
AFRICAN AMERICAN RELIGION Eddie S. Glaude Jr
AFRICAN HISTORY John Parker and Richard Rathbone
AFRICAN RELIGIONS Jacob K. Olupona
AGNOSTICISM Robin Le Poidevin
AGRICULTURE Paul Brassley and Richard Soffe
ALEXANDER THE GREAT Hugh Bowden
ALGEBRA Peter M. Higgins
AMERICAN HISTORY Paul S. Boyer
AMERICAN IMMIGRATION David A. Gerber
AMERICAN LEGAL HISTORY G. Edward White
AMERICAN POLITICAL HISTORY Donald Critchlow
AMERICAN POLITICAL PARTIES AND ELECTIONS L. Sandy Maisel
AMERICAN POLITICS Richard M. Valelly
THE AMERICAN PRESIDENCY Charles O. Jones
THE AMERICAN REVOLUTION Robert J. Allison
AMERICAN SLAVERY Heather Andrea Williams
THE AMERICAN WEST Stephen Aron
AMERICAN WOMEN'S HISTORY Susan Ware
ANAESTHESIA Aidan O'Donnell
ANARCHISM Colin Ward
ANCIENT ASSYRIA Karen Radner
ANCIENT EGYPT Ian Shaw
ANCIENT EGYPTIAN ART AND ARCHITECTURE Christina Riggs
ANCIENT GREECE Paul Cartledge
THE ANCIENT NEAR EAST Amanda H. Podany
ANCIENT PHILOSOPHY Julia Annas
ANCIENT WARFARE Harry Sidebottom
ANGELS David Albert Jones
ANGLICANISM Mark Chapman
THE ANGLO-SAXON AGE John Blair
THE ANIMAL KINGDOM Peter Holland
ANIMAL RIGHTS David DeGrazia
THE ANTARCTIC Klaus Dodds
ANTISEMITISM Steven Beller
ANXIETY Daniel Freeman and Jason Freeman
THE APOCRYPHAL GOSPELS Paul Foster
ARCHAEOLOGY Paul Bahn
ARCHITECTURE Andrew Ballantyne
ARISTOCRACY William Doyle
ARISTOTLE Jonathan Barnes
ART HISTORY Dana Arnold
ART THEORY Cynthia Freeland
ASTROBIOLOGY David C. Catling
ASTROPHYSICS James Binney
ATHEISM Julian Baggini
AUGUSTINE Henry Chadwick
AUSTRALIA Kenneth Morgan
AUTISM Uta Frith
THE AVANT GARDE David Cottington
THE AZTECS Davíd Carrasco
BABYLONIA Trevor Bryce

BACTERIA Sebastian G. B. Amyes
BARTHES Jonathan Culler
THE BEATS David Sterritt
BEAUTY Roger Scruton
BESTSELLERS John Sutherland
THE BIBLE John Riches
BIBLICAL ARCHAEOLOGY Eric H. Cline
BIOGRAPHY Hermione Lee
BLACK HOLES Katherine Blundell
BLOOD Chris Cooper
THE BLUES Elijah Wald
THE BODY Chris Shilling
THE BOOK OF MORMON Terryl Givens
BORDERS Alexander C. Diener and Joshua Hagen
THE BRAIN Michael O'Shea
THE BRICS Andrew F. Cooper
THE BRITISH CONSTITUTION Martin Loughlin
THE BRITISH EMPIRE Ashley Jackson
BRITISH POLITICS Anthony Wright
BUDDHA Michael Carrithers
BUDDHISM Damien Keown
BUDDHIST ETHICS Damien Keown
BYZANTIUM Peter Sarris
CANCER Nicholas James
CAPITALISM James Fulcher
CATHOLICISM Gerald O'Collins
CAUSATION Stephen Mumford and Rani Lill Anjum
THE CELL Terence Allen and Graham Cowling
THE CELTS Barry Cunliffe
CHAOS Leonard Smith
CHEMISTRY Peter Atkins
CHILD PSYCHOLOGY Usha Goswami
CHILDREN'S LITERATURE Kimberley Reynolds
CHINESE LITERATURE Sabina Knight
CHOICE THEORY Michael Allingham
CHRISTIAN ART Beth Williamson
CHRISTIAN ETHICS D. Stephen Long
CHRISTIANITY Linda Woodhead
CITIZENSHIP Richard Bellamy
CIVIL ENGINEERING David Muir Wood
CLASSICAL LITERATURE William Allan
CLASSICAL MYTHOLOGY Helen Morales
CLASSICS Mary Beard and John Henderson
CLAUSEWITZ Michael Howard
CLIMATE Mark Maslin
CLIMATE CHANGE Mark Maslin
THE COLD WAR Robert McMahon
COLONIAL AMERICA Alan Taylor
COLONIAL LATIN AMERICAN LITERATURE Rolena Adorno
COMBINATORICS Robin Wilson
COMEDY Matthew Bevis
COMMUNISM Leslie Holmes
COMPLEXITY John H. Holland
THE COMPUTER Darrel Ince
COMPUTER SCIENCE Subrata Dasgupta
CONFUCIANISM Daniel K. Gardner
THE CONQUISTADORS Matthew Restall and Felipe Fernández-Armesto
CONSCIENCE Paul Strohm
CONSCIOUSNESS Susan Blackmore
CONTEMPORARY ART Julian Stallabrass
CONTEMPORARY FICTION Robert Eaglestone
CONTINENTAL PHILOSOPHY Simon Critchley
COPERNICUS Owen Gingerich
CORAL REEFS Charles Sheppard
CORPORATE SOCIAL RESPONSIBILITY Jeremy Moon
CORRUPTION Leslie Holmes
COSMOLOGY Peter Coles
CRIME FICTION Richard Bradford
CRIMINAL JUSTICE Julian V. Roberts
CRITICAL THEORY Stephen Eric Bronner
THE CRUSADES Christopher Tyerman
CRYPTOGRAPHY Fred Piper and Sean Murphy
CRYSTALLOGRAPHY A. M. Glazer
THE CULTURAL REVOLUTION Richard Curt Kraus
DADA AND SURREALISM David Hopkins
DANTE Peter Hainsworth and David Robey
DARWIN Jonathan Howard
THE DEAD SEA SCROLLS Timothy Lim
DECOLONIZATION Dane Kennedy
DEMOCRACY Bernard Crick
DERRIDA Simon Glendinning
DESCARTES Tom Sorell
DESERTS Nick Middleton
DESIGN John Heskett

DEVELOPMENTAL BIOLOGY Lewis Wolpert
THE DEVIL Darren Oldridge
DIASPORA Kevin Kenny
DICTIONARIES Lynda Mugglestone
DINOSAURS David Norman
DIPLOMACY Joseph M. Siracusa
DOCUMENTARY FILM Patricia Aufderheide
DREAMING J. Allan Hobson
DRUGS Les Iversen
DRUIDS Barry Cunliffe
EARLY MUSIC Thomas Forrest Kelly
THE EARTH Martin Redfern
EARTH SYSTEM SCIENCE Tim Lenton
ECONOMICS Partha Dasgupta
EDUCATION Gary Thomas
EGYPTIAN MYTH Geraldine Pinch
EIGHTEENTH-CENTURY BRITAIN Paul Langford
THE ELEMENTS Philip Ball
EMOTION Dylan Evans
EMPIRE Stephen Howe
ENGELS Terrell Carver
ENGINEERING David Blockley
ENGLISH LITERATURE Jonathan Bate
THE ENLIGHTENMENT John Robertson
ENTREPRENEURSHIP Paul Westhead and Mike Wright
ENVIRONMENTAL ECONOMICS Stephen Smith
ENVIRONMENTAL POLITICS Andrew Dobson
EPICUREANISM Catherine Wilson
EPIDEMIOLOGY Rodolfo Saracci
ETHICS Simon Blackburn
ETHNOMUSICOLOGY Timothy Rice
THE ETRUSCANS Christopher Smith
THE EUROPEAN UNION John Pinder and Simon Usherwood
EVOLUTION Brian and Deborah Charlesworth
EXISTENTIALISM Thomas Flynn
EXPLORATION Stewart A. Weaver
THE EYE Michael Land
FAMILY LAW Jonathan Herring
FASCISM Kevin Passmore
FASHION Rebecca Arnold
FEMINISM Margaret Walters
FILM Michael Wood
FILM MUSIC Kathryn Kalinak
THE FIRST WORLD WAR Michael Howard
FOLK MUSIC Mark Slobin
FOOD John Krebs
FORENSIC PSYCHOLOGY David Canter
FORENSIC SCIENCE Jim Fraser
FORESTS Jaboury Ghazoul
FOSSILS Keith Thomson
FOUCAULT Gary Gutting
THE FOUNDING FATHERS R. B. Bernstein
FRACTALS Kenneth Falconer
FREE SPEECH Nigel Warburton
FREE WILL Thomas Pink
FRENCH LITERATURE John D. Lyons
THE FRENCH REVOLUTION William Doyle
FREUD Anthony Storr
FUNDAMENTALISM Malise Ruthven
FUNGI Nicholas P. Money
GALAXIES John Gribbin
GALILEO Stillman Drake
GAME THEORY Ken Binmore
GANDHI Bhikhu Parekh
GENES Jonathan Slack
GENIUS Andrew Robinson
GEOGRAPHY John Matthews and David Herbert
GEOPOLITICS Klaus Dodds
GERMAN LITERATURE Nicholas Boyle
GERMAN PHILOSOPHY Andrew Bowie
GLOBAL CATASTROPHES Bill McGuire
GLOBAL ECONOMIC HISTORY Robert C. Allen
GLOBALIZATION Manfred Steger
GOD John Bowker
GOETHE Ritchie Robertson
THE GOTHIC Nick Groom
GOVERNANCE Mark Bevir
THE GREAT DEPRESSION AND THE NEW DEAL Eric Rauchway
HABERMAS James Gordon Finlayson
HAPPINESS Daniel M. Haybron
THE HARLEM RENAISSANCE Cheryl A. Wall
THE HEBREW BIBLE AS LITERATURE Tod Linafelt
HEGEL Peter Singer

HEIDEGGER Michael Inwood
HERMENEUTICS Jens Zimmermann
HERODOTUS Jennifer T. Roberts
HIEROGLYPHS Penelope Wilson
HINDUISM Kim Knott
HISTORY John H. Arnold
THE HISTORY OF ASTRONOMY Michael Hoskin
THE HISTORY OF CHEMISTRY William H. Brock
THE HISTORY OF LIFE Michael Benton
THE HISTORY OF MATHEMATICS Jacqueline Stedall
THE HISTORY OF MEDICINE William Bynum
THE HISTORY OF TIME Leofranc Holford-Strevens
HIV/AIDS Alan Whiteside
HOBBES Richard Tuck
HOLLYWOOD Peter Decherney
HORMONES Martin Luck
HUMAN ANATOMY Leslie Klenerman
HUMAN EVOLUTION Bernard Wood
HUMAN RIGHTS Andrew Clapham
HUMANISM Stephen Law
HUME A. J. Ayer
HUMOUR Noël Carroll
THE ICE AGE Jamie Woodward
IDEOLOGY Michael Freeden
INDIAN CINEMA Ashish Rajadhyaksha
INDIAN PHILOSOPHY Sue Hamilton
INFECTIOUS DISEASE Marta L. Wayne and Benjamin M. Bolker
INFORMATION Luciano Floridi
INNOVATION Mark Dodgson and David Gann
INTELLIGENCE Ian J. Deary
INTERNATIONAL LAW Vaughan Lowe
INTERNATIONAL MIGRATION Khalid Koser
INTERNATIONAL RELATIONS Paul Wilkinson
INTERNATIONAL SECURITY Christopher S. Browning
IRAN Ali M. Ansari
ISLAM Malise Ruthven
ISLAMIC HISTORY Adam Silverstein
ISOTOPES Rob Ellam
ITALIAN LITERATURE Peter Hainsworth and David Robey
JESUS Richard Bauckham
JOURNALISM Ian Hargreaves
JUDAISM Norman Solomon
JUNG Anthony Stevens
KABBALAH Joseph Dan
KAFKA Ritchie Robertson
KANT Roger Scruton
KEYNES Robert Skidelsky
KIERKEGAARD Patrick Gardiner
KNOWLEDGE Jennifer Nagel
THE KORAN Michael Cook
LANDSCAPE ARCHITECTURE Ian H. Thompson
LANDSCAPES AND GEOMORPHOLOGY Andrew Goudie and Heather Viles
LANGUAGES Stephen R. Anderson
LATE ANTIQUITY Gillian Clark
LAW Raymond Wacks
THE LAWS OF THERMODYNAMICS Peter Atkins
LEADERSHIP Keith Grint
LEARNING Mark Haselgrove
LIBERALISM Michael Freeden
LIGHT Ian Walmsley
LINCOLN Allen C. Guelzo
LINGUISTICS Peter Matthews
LITERARY THEORY Jonathan Culler
LOCKE John Dunn
LOGIC Graham Priest
LOVE Ronald de Sousa
MACHIAVELLI Quentin Skinner
MADNESS Andrew Scull
MAGIC Owen Davies
MAGNA CARTA Nicholas Vincent
MAGNETISM Stephen Blundell
MALTHUS Donald Winch
MANAGEMENT John Hendry
MAO Delia Davin
MARINE BIOLOGY Philip V. Mladenov
THE MARQUIS DE SADE John Phillips
MARTIN LUTHER Scott H. Hendrix
MARTYRDOM Jolyon Mitchell
MARX Peter Singer
MATERIALS Christopher Hall
MATHEMATICS Timothy Gowers
THE MEANING OF LIFE Terry Eagleton
MEDICAL ETHICS Tony Hope
MEDICAL LAW Charles Foster

MEDIEVAL BRITAIN John Gillingham and Ralph A. Griffiths
MEDIEVAL LITERATURE Elaine Treharne
MEDIEVAL PHILOSOPHY John Marenbon
MEMORY Jonathan K. Foster
METAPHYSICS Stephen Mumford
THE MEXICAN REVOLUTION Alan Knight
MICHAEL FARADAY Frank A. J. L. James
MICROBIOLOGY Nicholas P. Money
MICROECONOMICS Avinash Dixit
MICROSCOPY Terence Allen
THE MIDDLE AGES Miri Rubin
MILITARY JUSTICE Eugene R. Fidell
MINERALS David Vaughan
MODERN ART David Cottington
MODERN CHINA Rana Mitter
MODERN DRAMA Kirsten E. Shepherd-Barr
MODERN FRANCE Vanessa R. Schwartz
MODERN IRELAND Senia Pašeta
MODERN JAPAN Christopher Goto-Jones
MODERN LATIN AMERICAN LITERATURE Roberto González Echevarría
MODERN WAR Richard English
MODERNISM Christopher Butler
MOLECULAR BIOLOGY Aysha Divan and Janice A. Royds
MOLECULES Philip Ball
THE MONGOLS Morris Rossabi
MOONS David A. Rothery
MORMONISM Richard Lyman Bushman
MOUNTAINS Martin F. Price
MUHAMMAD Jonathan A. C. Brown
MULTICULTURALISM Ali Rattansi
MUSIC Nicholas Cook
MYTH Robert A. Segal
THE NAPOLEONIC WARS Mike Rapport
NATIONALISM Steven Grosby
NELSON MANDELA Elleke Boehmer
NEOLIBERALISM Manfred Steger and Ravi Roy
NETWORKS Guido Caldarelli and Michele Catanzaro
THE NEW TESTAMENT Luke Timothy Johnson
THE NEW TESTAMENT AS LITERATURE Kyle Keefer
NEWTON Robert Iliffe
NIETZSCHE Michael Tanner
NINETEENTH-CENTURY BRITAIN Christopher Harvie and H. C. G. Matthew
THE NORMAN CONQUEST George Garnett
NORTH AMERICAN INDIANS Theda Perdue and Michael D. Green
NORTHERN IRELAND Marc Mulholland
NOTHING Frank Close
NUCLEAR PHYSICS Frank Close
NUCLEAR POWER Maxwell Irvine
NUCLEAR WEAPONS Joseph M. Siracusa
NUMBERS Peter M. Higgins
NUTRITION David A. Bender
OBJECTIVITY Stephen Gaukroger
THE OLD TESTAMENT Michael D. Coogan
THE ORCHESTRA D. Kern Holoman
ORGANIZATIONS Mary Jo Hatch
PAGANISM Owen Davies
THE PALESTINIAN-ISRAELI CONFLICT Martin Bunton
PARTICLE PHYSICS Frank Close
PAUL E. P. Sanders
PEACE Oliver P. Richmond
PENTECOSTALISM William K. Kay
THE PERIODIC TABLE Eric R. Scerri
PHILOSOPHY Edward Craig
PHILOSOPHY IN THE ISLAMIC WORLD Peter Adamson
PHILOSOPHY OF LAW Raymond Wacks
PHILOSOPHY OF SCIENCE Samir Okasha
PHOTOGRAPHY Steve Edwards
PHYSICAL CHEMISTRY Peter Atkins
PILGRIMAGE Ian Reader
PLAGUE Paul Slack
PLANETS David A. Rothery
PLANTS Timothy Walker
PLATE TECTONICS Peter Molnar
PLATO Julia Annas
POLITICAL PHILOSOPHY David Miller
POLITICS Kenneth Minogue
POSTCOLONIALISM Robert Young

POSTMODERNISM Christopher Butler
POSTSTRUCTURALISM Catherine Belsey
PREHISTORY Chris Gosden
PRESOCRATIC PHILOSOPHY Catherine Osborne
PRIVACY Raymond Wacks
PROBABILITY John Haigh
PROGRESSIVISM Walter Nugent
PROTESTANTISM Mark A. Noll
PSYCHIATRY Tom Burns
PSYCHOANALYSIS Daniel Pick
PSYCHOLOGY Gillian Butler and Freda McManus
PSYCHOTHERAPY Tom Burns and Eva Burns-Lundgren
PUBLIC ADMINISTRATION Stella Z. Theodoulou and Ravi K. Roy
PUBLIC HEALTH Virginia Berridge
PURITANISM Francis J. Bremer
THE QUAKERS Pink Dandelion
QUANTUM THEORY John Polkinghorne
RACISM Ali Rattansi
RADIOACTIVITY Claudio Tuniz
RASTAFARI Ennis B. Edmonds
THE REAGAN REVOLUTION Gil Troy
REALITY Jan Westerhoff
THE REFORMATION Peter Marshall
RELATIVITY Russell Stannard
RELIGION IN AMERICA Timothy Beal
THE RENAISSANCE Jerry Brotton
RENAISSANCE ART Geraldine A. Johnson
REVOLUTIONS Jack A. Goldstone
RHETORIC Richard Toye
RISK Baruch Fischhoff and John Kadvany
RITUAL Barry Stephenson
RIVERS Nick Middleton
ROBOTICS Alan Winfield
ROMAN BRITAIN Peter Salway
THE ROMAN EMPIRE Christopher Kelly
THE ROMAN REPUBLIC David M. Gwynn
ROMANTICISM Michael Ferber
ROUSSEAU Robert Wokler
RUSSELL A. C. Grayling
RUSSIAN HISTORY Geoffrey Hosking
RUSSIAN LITERATURE Catriona Kelly
THE RUSSIAN REVOLUTION S. A. Smith
SAVANNA Peter A. Furley
SCHIZOPHRENIA Chris Frith and Eve Johnstone
SCHOPENHAUER Christopher Janaway
SCIENCE AND RELIGION Thomas Dixon
SCIENCE FICTION David Seed
THE SCIENTIFIC REVOLUTION Lawrence M. Principe
SCOTLAND Rab Houston
SEXUALITY Véronique Mottier
SHAKESPEARE'S COMEDIES Bart van Es
SIKHISM Eleanor Nesbitt
THE SILK ROAD James A. Millward
SLANG Jonathon Green
SLEEP Steven W. Lockley and Russell G. Foster
SOCIAL AND CULTURAL ANTHROPOLOGY John Monaghan and Peter Just
SOCIAL PSYCHOLOGY Richard J. Crisp
SOCIAL WORK Sally Holland and Jonathan Scourfield
SOCIALISM Michael Newman
SOCIOLINGUISTICS John Edwards
SOCIOLOGY Steve Bruce
SOCRATES C. C. W. Taylor
SOUND Mike Goldsmith
THE SOVIET UNION Stephen Lovell
THE SPANISH CIVIL WAR Helen Graham
SPANISH LITERATURE Jo Labanyi
SPINOZA Roger Scruton
SPIRITUALITY Philip Sheldrake
SPORT Mike Cronin
STARS Andrew King
STATISTICS David J. Hand
STEM CELLS Jonathan Slack
STRUCTURAL ENGINEERING David Blockley
STUART BRITAIN John Morrill
SUPERCONDUCTIVITY Stephen Blundell
SYMMETRY Ian Stewart
TAXATION Stephen Smith
TEETH Peter S. Ungar
TERRORISM Charles Townshend
THEATRE Marvin Carlson
THEOLOGY David F. Ford
THOMAS AQUINAS Fergus Kerr
THOUGHT Tim Bayne

Chris Cooper

BLOOD

A Very Short Introduction

OXFORD
UNIVERSITY PRESS

OXFORD
UNIVERSITY PRESS

Great Clarendon Street, Oxford, OX2 6DP,
United Kingdom

Oxford University Press is a department of the University of Oxford.
It furthers the University's objective of excellence in research, scholarship,
and education by publishing worldwide. Oxford is a registered trade mark of
Oxford University Press in the UK and in certain other countries

First edition published in 2016

Impression: 1

Published in the United States of America by Oxford University Press
198 Madison Avenue, New York, NY 10016, United States of America

British Library Cataloguing in Publication Data
Data available

Library of Congress Control Number: 2016935943

ISBN 978–0–19–958145–0

Printed in Great Britain by
Ashford Colour Press Ltd, Gosport, Hampshire

To my father David Cooper (1935–2009) who taught me to question and my PhD supervisor Peter Nicholls (1935–2014) who taught me how to answer.

Contents

Conflict of interest: *The author has patents and shares in a spin out company seeking to develop a safe haemoglobin-based blood substitute.*

Acknowledgements

I am grateful for the support of the many scientists who suggested improvements to the first draft of this book. These include: Mervyn Singer and David Highton (both at University College London) who particularly helped with the chapters on blood pressure, blood flow, and blood transfusion; Mike Wilson (University of Essex) who contributed many interesting stories about haemoglobin; and Nelson Fernandez (also University of Essex) who was a great support in the writing of the immunology section. I would also like to thank the three anonymous readers of the initial proposal for many pertinent suggestions. It goes without saying that any remaining scientific errors are my own fault.

My wife, Helen Cooper, provided the valuable insights of an intelligent non-scientist. At Oxford University Press, Jenny Nugee and Latha Menon provided advice on content and assisted in technical aspects of the book's production.

Finally writing a book is a time consuming and emotional commitment. I could not have succeeded without the support of my family especially my mother Maria, my wife Helen, and my two children Alex and Lauren.

List of illustrations

Chapter 1
A history of blood

Blood as metaphor

Blood and blood metaphors are intrinsic to our language. Red is a universal symbol for danger. Your lifeblood drains away; when you are angry you see red, whether in William Makepeace Thackeray's *The Virginians* (1857), 'A choking, dreadful feeling arrested my breath; the ground rocked beneath my feet; a red mist swam before my eyes' or in Nick Hornby's *Fever Pitch* (2002), 'Shortly before his goal against Newcastle, one of the frequent red mists that plagued him had descended, and he had grabbed a rugged Newcastle defender by the throat and lifted him from the ground'. This is partly physiological—blood flow being redirected to the skin does indeed make you red-faced when you are angry—but also has its roots in the crucial importance of blood to life. If you are really angry your blood 'boils over' with rage.

Yet some have suggested that blood, the colour red, and danger were not always so closely linked. Gladstone, four times British prime minister during the reign of Queen Victoria, was a noted scholar of Greek mythology. In 1858, in *Studies on Homer and the Homeric Age* he noted that that there was virtually no incidence of colour in Homer's works, beyond differing shades of light and dark. He suggested that Ancient Greeks were colour blind and that is why there was no colour in their language. The concept seems bizarre to us. Steeped in modern European languages, it seems inconceivable to us that in some tongues it is not possible to ask the question 'What colour is it?'. Yet this is indeed the case. Languages can be grouped according to the number and types of colours they describe. There have been attempts to correlate the emergence of a specific colour in language with the evolution of the physiology or neurophysiology able to describe it. Some even suggest that without a language for colour that colour can't be perceived. Without getting into the fine details of this on-going debate, it is generally agreed that if any language has a word for a colour other than black and white, that colour is red. And as black and white correspond to light and dark, red may be said to be the true first colour of language and thought.

For biophysicists used to discussing colour quantitatively in terms of wavelengths of light, the idea that a colour might not exist until it is described in language appears odd. But a relatively recent example illustrates this perfectly. On 4 June 1859, the French army under Napoleon III defeated the Austrians in a battle fought just outside Milan in Italy. At the same time as this battle a synthetic dye was being designed by two British chemists in south London, Edward Nicholson and George Maule. They originally named their dye 'roseine'. However, they changed the name to that of the small town where this battle was fought, allegedly noting that their new dye was the same colour as the mixture of red blood with the blue uniforms of the wounded French Zouave soldiers. The town was called 'Magenta'. The colour does not occur 'naturally' in a rainbow, being a mixture of red and blue light in the absence of green. Still, even if Nicolson and Maule had never existed, the modern age would have required its invention. Magenta is a key component of colour printing, being one of the three subtractive primary colours, along with yellow and cyan. Mixtures of these three were first used in newspaper colour comic strips in the 1890s, though most of us are more familiar with them in the colour ink cartridges we buy for our digital printers.

It is not difficult to see why the colour red holds such pre-eminence in human language and culture. We are fascinated by orifices and the bodily fluids that emerge from them. These provide the direct link between the person and the environment. An individual's tears, urine, saliva, semen, and faeces have all been historically invested with powerful properties. But from the most basic hunter to the child savaged by a prehistoric predator, it is clear that blood was the most powerful fluid. Only the red fluid flowed freely in large volumes; only its loss led to death. Blood pumps out of the heart of the slaughtered animal; when the heart stops, the flow ceases: life ends. Conversely, when a young woman stops losing blood every month, it is a sign that a new life is beginning.

Blood features in powerful rituals, both religious and of more general cultural significance. The ancient Mayans believed that the gods used their own blood to create human beings (in return, the humans sacrificed blood to placate the gods). Sumerians believed a mixture of blood and clay was used. It was once a commonly held belief that the foetus was formed from menstrual blood; in the absence of other evidence this was a perfectly sensible hypothesis given that menstruation stops during pregnancy and that the end of menstruation (the menopause) signifies that a woman has passed her childbearing age.

The view that blood is life-giving is widespread. In Greek mythology Odysseus is able to briefly revive the dead in Hades by giving them blood to drink; and while the blood from the veins on the left side of the snake-headed Gorgon Medusa was deadly, the blood from the right side was life-giving. The hero Perseus slew Medusa, using the reflecting shield of the goddess Athena to avoid being turned to stone by her deadly gaze. In one version of the myth, Athena claimed her reward by taking some of Medusa's blood (from the veins on the right, of course) and giving it to her son, Asclepius. Asclepius consequently became a great healer, even able to raise the dead. The first line of the original version of the doctor's Hippocratic oath requires the physician to swear, not just to Apollo the physician, but also to the surgeon Asclepius and his daughters Hygieia and Panacea.

Most cultures, ancient and modern, have foodstuffs made up of blood, from Britain's regional black pudding delicacy to the Ñachi of the Mapuche, the indigenous peoples of southern Chile and southwestern Argentina. The blood of the Roman gladiators, mopped up with a sponge, fed a profitable business. But the benefits of blood eating were not merely nutritional. Drinking fresh blood was supposed to give you strength or, in the case of vampire myths, eternal life. Even in the post-enlightenment age, the first blood transfusions had nothing to do with our modern notion of supporting oxygen supply; instead they were supposed to cure a sick patient's ailment by replacing their old bad blood with strong healthy animal blood.

Native North American cultures talk about hunted animals being re-formed from the blood spilled at the scene of the kill. Blood is frequently thought to contain a person's spirit. In Central Africa, there was a resistance to colonial attempts to introduce blood transfusions in the 1950s, because it meant replacing your spirit with someone else's. Over five million Jehovah's Witnesses believe that blood represents life and so refuse transfusions. Over one billion Roman Catholics believe that eating the body and drinking the blood of Christ in Holy Communion is the channel to eternal life ('he who eats my flesh and drinks my blood has eternal life, and I will raise him up at the last day' (John 6:54)).

The use of blood in rituals can be part of the process of initiation. The Ndrangheta mafia have a pledge of 'blood and honour' which involves the initiate cutting himself with a knife and using his blood in the ceremony. Two people can bond by mixing their blood together, becoming 'blood brothers' in the process. One of the earliest descriptions is in Norse mythology when, following two days of fighting, the Norwegian warrior Örvar-Oddr and the

Swedish warrior Hjalmar agreed a draw by letting their blood flow together on to the ground. In more modern times the siblings-to-be press cuts together to exchange their blood.

The symbolism of blood exchange creating a fraternal bond requires a belief that natural brothers share kinship through their blood. Indeed 'blood brothers' can just as well mean natural brothers as those bonded by ritual. For most of human history, blood not DNA was the essence of life and hence, *de facto*, the agent of heredity. The metaphors are rich: bloodstock, bloodline, blood tie.

Yet the spirit that occupies blood is not always considered so benign. In some cultures blood is feared, and there is a taboo against spilling it. The blood of the wounded and dying on battlefields would leave them barren. The blood of leaders was especially potent; the Betsileo, a highland ethnic group of Madagascar, protected their leaders with a slave tasked with licking up any blood before it reached the ground. A staggering variety of cultures and religions consider menstruating women to be unclean. Frequently isolated from communities in menstrual huts, prohibitions have included not bathing, eating only at night, not making contact with things associated with men, and, of course, refraining from sexual intercourse. The Roman scholar Pliny's *Natural History* informed the reader that a menstruating woman could blight plants through her breath or kill insects merely by walking through a field. In the 13th century Rabbi Nahmanides stated that, 'She is a pariah . . . the dust on which she walks is impure like the dust defiled by the bones of the dead'. Not to be outdone, an infamous medieval Christian tome *De secretis mulierum* (*On the Secrets of Women*) opined that 'Women are so full of venom at the time of menstruation that they poison animals by their glare, they infect children in the cradle, they spot the cleanest mirror'. In the 20th century this was given a scientific gloss under the guise of 'menotoxin', a toxin present in menstrual blood and, sometimes, in the sweat of menstruating women. This topic was actively debated in the letters pages of the famous medical journal, *The Lancet*, even as recently as 1977.

Blood in medicine

The importance of blood in history and culture is universal. Yet the views about what function it actually performed in the body have varied widely. The Ancient Greeks considered the world made up of four elements: earth, air, fire, and water. Hippocrates—he of the doctor's oath—sought to integrate this idea with what was known of the body. The power of four was key to their thinking. Undigested food was converted to 'humours' that needed to be eliminated lest they cause disease. Phlegm came from the brain, while the liver produced black bile, and spleen yellow bile. But this made only three. To make up a fourth humour, blood was added. Coming from the heart—the thinking organ—blood differed from the other humours in having a generally positive effect in the body. Just like today, blood was thought of as the body's transportation system. It communicated with the four elements in the world outside, bringing the different systems into balance. This blood-centred view of life was taken to the extreme by Aristotle, who associated blood with mental as well as physical health—for example, a person with 'thin blood' would necessarily be timid.

Once the nature of blood was linked with disease, therapies emerged. Of the four humours, blood provided heat and humidity. Therefore drinking wine to warm up a cold person must be due to an increase in the amount of their blood. Building up blood is also the purpose behind many medicinal plants used in traditional medicine in sub-Saharan Africa. Some of these plants have been shown to be rich in iron, thus providing a modern scientific basis for their use in the treatment of anaemia. The same cannot be said for 'wheatgrass therapy'. This is an alternative therapy in modern Western societies that assumes the similarities in the chemical structure of the green magnesium pigment in plants (chlorophyll) to the red iron pigment in animals (haem) means that ingesting wheatgrass juice can increase the number of red blood cells in the body.

In the centuries following Aristotle, medicine turned away from building up blood; instead, blood was to be eliminated—a process called 'bloodletting'. This mistake was not rectified until the success of transfusion science in the 20th century. Why did removing this life-giving substance become such a key part of medicine? Again it related to humours. Natural bloodletting such as menstruation and nosebleeds were the body's way of restoring the balance of the elements; therefore directed bloodletting by a physician could be of use in the wide variety of illnesses caused by a misbalance of the humours.

The removal of blood as a therapy became entrenched following the work of the 2nd-century physician, Galen. At the time there were strong taboos about dissecting the human body; Galen waxes lyrical about the opportunity offered to him when a flooded river deposited a dead body from a nearby grave for him to study. This contrasted with the anatomist Erasistratus, who practised in Syria some 500 years earlier and was allowed to dissect the bodies of living criminals. Still, in his later role as physician to the gladiators, Galen no doubt had ample opportunity to observe directly the wounded human body, even if he could not control the nature of the incisions made.

Most of Galen's dogmatic—and scientifically untested—treatises are the polar opposite of what we would today call evidence-based medicine. His views of anatomy held sway from the 2nd century until well into the 16th. Bloodletting itself, either directly or via the use of bloodsucking insects such as leeches, was still being practised up until the early 20th century. Its most notable victim was the first US president, George Washington, who had almost half his total blood volume removed as a treatment for inflammation of the epiglottis. Galen believed an overabundance of blood humour was a primary cause of illness, bloodletting being the obvious cure. In this he differed from the followers of Erasistratus, who held court in Rome at the time. In one famous case described by Galen, a woman with suppressed menstruation who had a cough, shortness of breath, and a red face was refused bloodletting by her physicians—she died suffocating and coughing up blood. It is not difficult to see how this could be interpreted as a last ditch attempt by her body to rid itself of excess blood humour, thus strengthening Galen's views about the benefits of preventative bloodletting.

Bloodletting (technically termed 'phlebotomy') is a niche therapy in modern Western medicine. It is reserved for conditions in which iron (hemochromatosis, porphyria cutanea tarda) or red blood cells (polycythemia vera) accumulate to dangerous levels. Removing these cells and the iron they contain therefore makes good medical sense. In the last twenty-five years leech therapy has made a comeback, but again in niche treatments such as microsurgery, where they can temporarily prevent the build-up of blood and blood clotting in difficult-to-access areas.

Apart from these rare situations, modern blood medicine has little to learn from the likes of Erasistratus and Galen. Indeed it is only in recent centuries that active interventions by physicians have been generally beneficial; as for the unfortunate Washington, most pre-20th-century interventions were actively harmful. This contrasts with the debt we owe these early scholars for the state of our current knowledge of the function of blood and blood circulation, even if the route of travel from Galen to the modern day has been somewhat circuitous.

A renaissance in blood biology

The structure of the vessels that contain blood in the body—our arteries and veins—has always intrigued scholars. In fact, Erasistratus came quite close to the truth. He noted that there appeared to be a connection between veins and arteries, possibly where they met in the heart. The basic structure of a circulation system can be gleaned when looking back on his work. However, its function remained obscure, in part because Erasistratus thought arteries were full of air, not blood. Galen, on the other hand, understood that both arteries and veins were full of blood; he even recognized that blood in the arteries was bright red and that in the veins more purple in hue. But he did not think that blood circulated. Instead he argued that blood was produced by the liver and consumed by the rest of the body. In a statement even a modern physiologist would agree with, Galen claimed that the liver received food nutrients from the gut via the hepatic portal vein. However, this goodness was then converted into nutritive blood. Nutritive blood then went on its one-way journey in the venous system to the rest of the body where it was consumed.

What about the role of the lungs? These were key to the other transportation system in the body. In Galen's view, air was drawn into the lungs and its vital spirit (*pneuma*) mixed with the blood. This red *vivified blood* was then passed around the body via the arteries. The role of the heart was to transfer the purple nutritive blood from the liver to the lungs, where it could be converted into vivified blood. The arteries and veins therefore performed two different roles. The blood in arteries conveyed the vital spirit from air while the blood in veins moved nutrients around the body. Of course, moving food and oxygen gas around the body are indeed the main roles for blood. Galen just failed to make the connection that they travelled in the same closed system. And to be fair why should he have made such a connection? Blood in arteries and blood in veins are very different colours. Arteries have thick elastic walls and can pulse, whereas veins are thin and cannot. Although he did note that there appeared to be some connections between the arterial and venous systems (we would now call these 'anastomoses' or 'shunts') he did not believe they were of any importance. The key connection—the capillaries—would remain invisible to anatomists until the great microscopist Marcel Malpighi successfully visualized them in 1661.

However, even before Malpighi the English physician William Harvey used astute measurements and calculations to make the connection between arteries and veins. In the process he correctly described the modern circulatory system. But before we get to his 1628 revolutionary book *De Motu Cordis* (*On the Motion of the Heart*) we should first look at the early attempts in the Renaissance world to interpret the blood system. The Renaissance saw a revolution in both science and art, with some individuals, notably Leonardo da Vinci, moving freely between them. Like many of his contemporaries, da Vinci tried to portray the world realistically rather than figuratively. This extended to the human body; although not medically qualified, da Vinci performed many autopsies ranging from a 2-year-old child to a 100-year-old man—this no doubt informed his scientific views on the heart.

Da Vinci's famous 1490 drawing of the human body's proportions, known as the 'Vitruvian Man', is hidden away in the Gallerie dell'Accademia in Venice (although you can see its image on the Italian €1 coin). Even more difficult to access until recently, and unpublished in his day, da Vinci drew over 200 highly detailed sketches of the human body based on his dissections of animals and people. These sketches found their way by a circuitous route to the art collection of the British royal family, where they lay largely unnoticed for over 400 years. What these drawings reveal is a level of technical detail that was astonishing for its time and well beyond anything Galen and his followers could have achieved. Possibly influenced by da Vinci, the Belgian physician Vesalius published his highly influential book on human anatomy, *De Humani Corporis Fabrica*.

Yet, despite their advances in understanding of the structure of the heart, da Vinci and Vesalius were merely tinkering with the Galenic worldview, modifying and updating the fine details. To both men the heart was still a muscle that was fed by arteries and veins; although the source of the mysterious pulse, it was by no means a circulatory pump. In the West, this idea would have to wait over a hundred years until Harvey's book was published. However, Harvey did not originate the idea of the heart as a pump; that pre-dated the Renaissance. For between what Europeans now call the Dark Ages and the Renaissance, advance in scientific thought was largely the domain of Islamic scholars.

The precise link between the 'discoveries' of the Renaissance and earlier Islamic science is controversial: how much was re-invention and how much re-interpretation is not always clear. However, in the field of anatomy, it is clear that the early 13th-century Islamic physician Ibn al-Nafis was the first to propose a circulatory system. The human heart has two upper chambers (right and left atrium) and two lower chambers (right and left ventricles). A complex system of thick walled vessels (called 'arteries'), thinner walled vessels (called 'veins') and valves was attached to these chambers (Figure 1). Galen claimed blood passed directly from the left to right chambers of the heart via invisible pores (the air passing to the left chamber as a gas in the pulmonary vein). Unlike Galen, al-Nafis considered that the pulmonary vein carried blood not air. As an anatomist, he then took his inability to see pores between the left and right chambers to its logical conclusion and suggested blood flowed from the right chamber of the heart via the pulmonary artery to the lungs, where it mixed with air, returning to the left chamber of the heart via the pulmonary vein. This is the first description of what we would now call the pulmonary (or lesser) circulation. However, Ibn al-Nafis maintained Galen's view that the vital spirit was made in the left chamber of the heart. The idea of a part of the air transferring to the blood in the lungs did not seem to occur to him. Perhaps this was not too surprising. For the discovery of oxygen—the invisible gas that is transported from the air to our body's cells via the lungs and blood circulation—was still five centuries away.

The structure of the heart

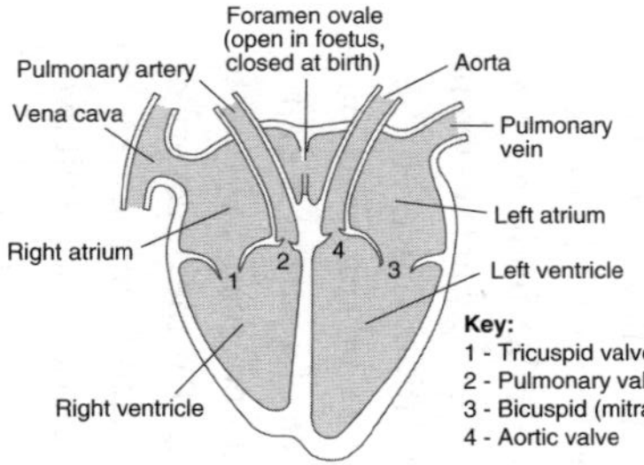

Key:
1 - Tricuspid valve
2 - Pulmonary valve
3 - Bicuspid (mitral) valve
4 - Aortic valve

Galen's view of blood circulation in the heart

Blood passes between right and left ventricles through invisible pores: when blood meets air it becomes mixed with the 'vital spirit'

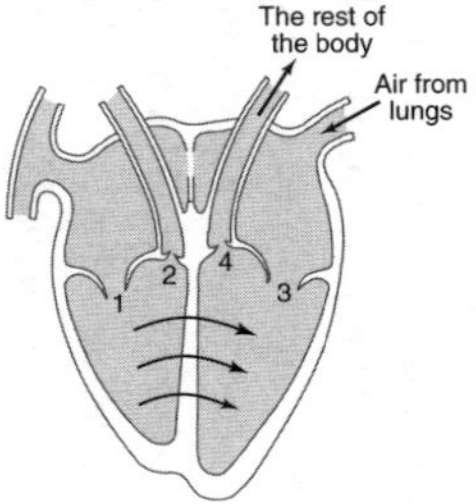

The lesser pulmonary circulation (Ibn al-Nafis)

Blood flows from the heart, through the lungs and returns to the heart. However this (pulmonary) 'closed' circulation is only secondary. The primary circulation is still thought to be 'open' with the blood being produced by the liver and consumed by the rest of the body.

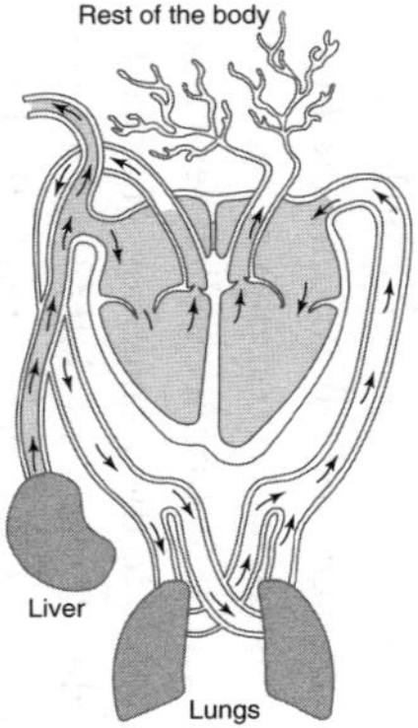

Harvey's (modern) view of blood circulation

Blood flows in a single closed circuit. Arteries take blood away from the heart and veins return blood back to the heart. The secondary pulmonary circulation takes blood between the heart and the lungs where it picks up oxygen from the air. The oxygenated blood is then passed around the body.

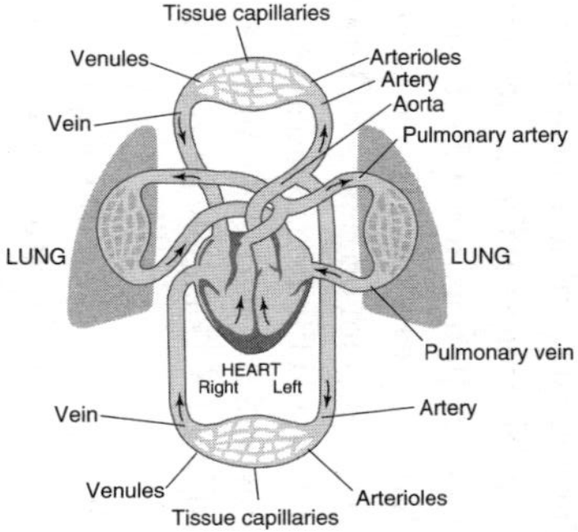

1. Ancient and modern views of blood circulation.

Ibn al-Nafis's split with Galen can still be viewed as evolutionary, rather than revolutionary. Like Galen, he assumed that blood was being continually made in the liver and flowed slowly around the body delivering nutrients and vital spirit along the way. Independently (as far as we know) of Ibn al-Nafis, two 17th-century scholars, Michael Servetus and Realdo Columbo, also described the lesser circulation of the heart/lung. Servetus's work was largely hidden from his peers and made little impact. This is not surprising. Although a physician, Servetus was far more concerned with religion than medicine or science. Consequently his ideas on the pulmonary circulation were never given prominence in his writing.

The relative importance of Servetus's scientific and religious studies can be debated. However, there is no debate about which was more dangerous to his health. His views on the Christian trinity, hell, and infant baptism managed to simultaneously outrage both the Catholic and Protestant churches. His work describing the pulmonary circulation was hidden in the pages of his last book *Christianismi Restitutio* (*The Restoration of Christianity*). This book was the last straw for many of his detractors, who included among their number the Catholics in the French inquisition and the founder of modern day Presbyterianism, John Calvin. Servetus was sentenced to death by the Roman Catholic authorities in Vienna in April 1553. Fleeing from jail, an effigy—along with his books—was burned in his place. This only proved a brief respite for Servetus, however, who was stopped in Geneva, a Calvinist stronghold. Although the Catholics demanded his return, the Protestants were unwilling to let him go. Instead, urged on by Calvin, they showed their religious zeal by burning him at the stake themselves, allegedly with the last copy of his book at his side. However, at least three copies of *Christianismi Restitutio* survived. Along with his scientific prescience, they illustrate his importance in the development of modern non-trinitarian Christian faiths such as Unitarians, Jehovah's Witnesses, and Oneness Pentecostalists.

The fame of the Italian anatomist and surgeon Columbo also rests on a single work, *De Re Anatomica*. This was published in 1559, six years after Servetus died. However, as Servetus's books were assumed to have all been burned by then it is not clear whether Columbo knew of his very similar ideas. During his vivisections of animals, Columbo always found blood in the pulmonary vein. Therefore like Servetus and Ibn al-Nafis before him, he was almost forced into describing the pulmonary circulation as the only sensible alternative. Unlike Ibn al-Nafis, Columbo suggests that the 'spirit' vivifies the blood as it passes through the lungs, not as it is later mixed in the heart. Replace spirit with oxygen and we can see 17th-century science edging ever closer to our modern interpretation of the function of the lungs in the circulatory system.

Columbo's work resonated with his peers and later scientists. His books are known to have been read by, and probably influenced, Harvey. They may well have been read by the Italian physician, philosopher, and botanist, Andrea Cesalpino, who in two books published at the end of the 16th century came very close to our modern understanding of the blood circulation. However, that scientific leap is today attributed to Harvey, in large part because of the clarity of his writings and their underpinning by scientific experiments and calculations.

Harvey's modern view of blood

William Harvey was born in 1578; in 1617 he became physician to the English king, James I (James VI of Scotland) and, subsequently, his son Charles I. Despite his close association with and enthusiasm for the Royalist cause in the English Civil War, he was able to remain active in science, publishing key works on the circulation of blood even in the year 1649, when Charles was executed and the Crown abolished. However, his magnum opus was published earlier, in 1628, and changed forever the scientific view of blood. Entitled *Exercitatio Anatomica de Motu Cordis et*

Sanguinis in Animalibus (*An Anatomical Exercise on the Motion of the Heart and Blood in Living Beings*), usually abbreviated to *de Motu Cordis*, it encapsulated views Harvey had been gestating over the previous ten years.

What were the key ideas that led Harvey to his view that blood transportation was a closed circuit, with the heart pumping the blood around the body in arteries, before it returned via the veins? Harvey was first able to determine exactly what happened when the heart beats. This happens so fast to the naked eye that he had to use cold-blooded animals (whose hearts generally beat more slowly) or animals close to death when the heart rate slows down. From these studies Harvey concluded that, in contrast to Galen's view, the heart did not attract blood to it. Instead it expelled it, the atria pushing blood to the ventricles. These, in turn, expelled the blood into the arteries. Arteries did not pulse of their own accord. Instead the 'pulse of the arteries is nothing but the implosion of blood into the arteries'.

Armed with this new knowledge of the motion of the heart, a true circulation system could be envisaged. All veins had valves but these were absent in arteries. The valves enabled venous blood to flow in one direction only, towards the heart. The absence of such valves in the arteries, and their thicker walls, suggested a higher pressure in the arteries. This all seemed consistent with a pressure-driven unidirectional flow of blood from arteries to veins. Harvey confirmed this by performing a number of studies on human volunteers. For example a cuff can be applied to the arm, as occurs when you have your blood pressure taken. If a low pressure is applied the hand becomes flushed with blood and the veins distended. Harvey interpreted this as blood flowing from the arteries into the veins, but not being able to leave due to an occlusion of the venous system. Applying an even higher pressure occludes the arterial system. Now there is no increase in blood volume, so the hand does not change colour and the veins do not distend. Blood cannot flow into or out of the hand. A pulse is only felt with the venous occlusion, linking the pulse to the flow of blood in the arteries. The simplest explanation is that the pulse is linked to the higher pressure in the arteries, which carry blood from the heart to the rest of the body where it is transferred to, and returned to the heart, via the venous system.

When experiments needed to be more invasive, Harvey was allowed privileged access, because of his position, to the royal deer. He severed veins to see which direction blood flowed, to or away from the heart. He also tied off arteries and veins to measure which side became engorged with blood and which side denuded. This indicated clearly the direction of flow and even a rough estimate of the flow rate could be made. It was for a version of this calculation with regards to the heart that Harvey is perhaps best remembered.

Harvey estimated the volume of the left chamber (ventricle) of the human heart when it was relaxed and when it was contracted. The difference (0.5 ounces of blood) is the amount pumped with each beat. Assuming 1,000 beats per half hour—a conservative estimate—this would mean that 500 ounces of blood would be pumped out of the heart in this time. In modern terms this would equate to about 0.5 kg of blood pumped per minute. But there is only 5 kg of total blood in the body. Therefore Galen's idea of a slow one-way movement of blood around the body is untenable. In Harvey's own words 'It is manifest that more blood is continually transmitted through the heart than either the food we receive can furnish or is possible to be contained in the veins'.

Harvey therefore clearly demonstrated that blood flowed through the heart in two separate closed loops. One, the pulmonary circulation, connected the circulatory system to the lungs. The other, the systemic circulation, caused blood to flow to the body's other organs and tissues. The modern blood circulation system had arrived. In Chapter 2 we shall explore what this system carries in more detail.

Chapter 2
What is blood?

Blood is special. Indeed in his tragedy *Faust*, Goethe has the devil himself state that 'Blut ist ein ganz besonderer Saft'—'blood is a juice of rarest quality'. However, beyond tasting metallic and being vital for life, the first humans had little idea about its composition. What they did know is that, left outside the body, it congealed into a solid clot within minutes. But they had no way of analysing this clot, or the fluid that surrounded it (now called 'serum') in detail. As early as the 4th century BC, Hippocrates realized that the clot was important to prevent excessive bleeding. For removing a scab, as any young boy will tell you, re-starts the bleeding process. However, the presence of a clot makes it difficult to study the components of blood. It also makes it impossible to store blood for transfusion. So there was a need to find a way to prevent clotting. Fortunately the discovery that the metal calcium accelerated the rate of clotting enabled the development of a range of compounds that bound calcium and therefore prevented this process. One of them, citrate, is still in common use today when blood is being prepared for storage, or to stop blood from clotting while it is being pumped through kidney dialysis machines and other extracorporeal circuits.

Adding citrate to blood, and leaving it alone, will result in gravity gradually separating the blood into three layers; the

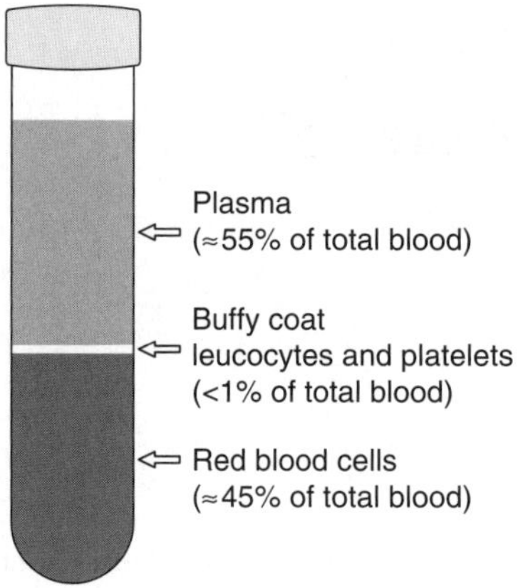

2. Composition of blood.

process can be accelerated by rapid spinning in a centrifuge (Figure 2). The top layer is clear and pale yellow or straw-coloured in appearance. This is the plasma, and it contains no cells. The bottom layer is bright red and contains the dense pellet of red cells that have sunk to the bottom of the tube. In-between these two layers is a very narrow layer, called the 'buffy coat' because of its pale yellow-brown appearance. This contains white blood cells and platelets. Although the fluid in which these cells swim—the plasma—is critical to the functioning of blood and its role in the body, to a haematologist it is the cells themselves that generally matter. These three cell types—red cells, white cells, and platelets—define the primary functions of blood: oxygen transport, immune defence, and coagulation. All the cells in the blood are made from one type of stem cell—the haematopoietic stem cell (Figure 3). This transformation happens in the bone marrow, which is found in the core of most bones. As the blood cells develop they seep into the blood that passes through the bones and hence enter the bloodstream.

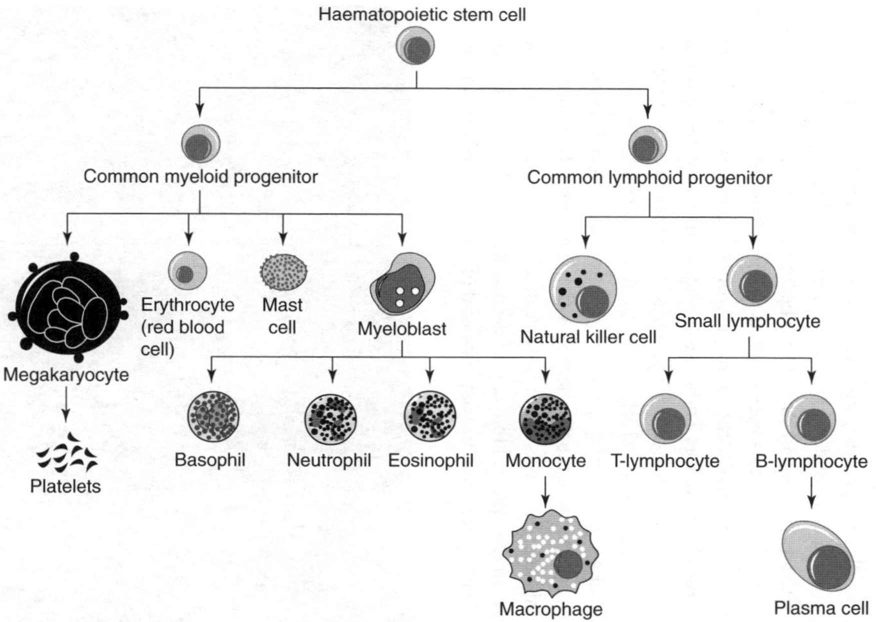

3. Developmental pathways of blood cells in the bone marrow.

Red cells

When viewed down a simple microscope, the general perception of cells is of static objects with a black blob in the middle (the nucleus). In fact cells are dynamic, mobile, three-dimensional structures, many of which are not restricted to a single nucleus. Cells vary dramatically in size and structure. The longest cell in the body is the neurone, which carries nerve impulses. These can reach over 1 metre in length, in particular the motor neurones that can run all the way from spinal cord to toe. These are closely followed by the sartorial muscle cell, so named as it is the one a tailor uses to determine an inside measurement, which can reach 60 cm in length. However, these cells are very thin; in terms of volume, the egg cell (ovum) is the largest, being almost spherical with a diameter of about a tenth of a millimetre. This is about the size of a sharp pencil point, making the ovum the only cell that can be seen with the naked eye. The red blood cell comes in at the opposite end of the scale, being only about

(a)

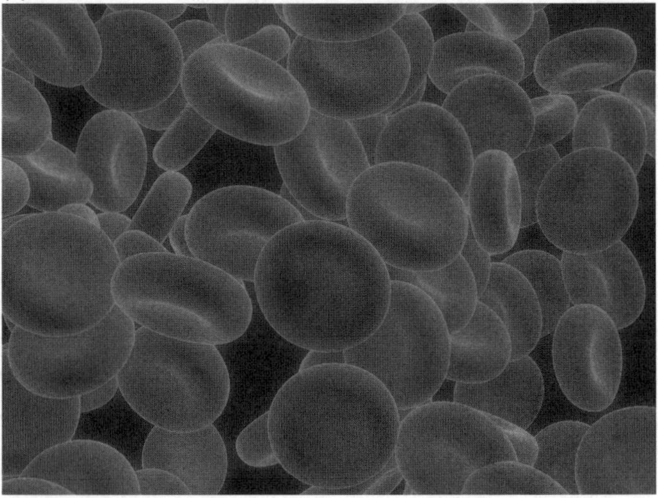

4. Shape of red blood cells. (a) Biconcave flexible disks can squeeze through narrow openings

(b)

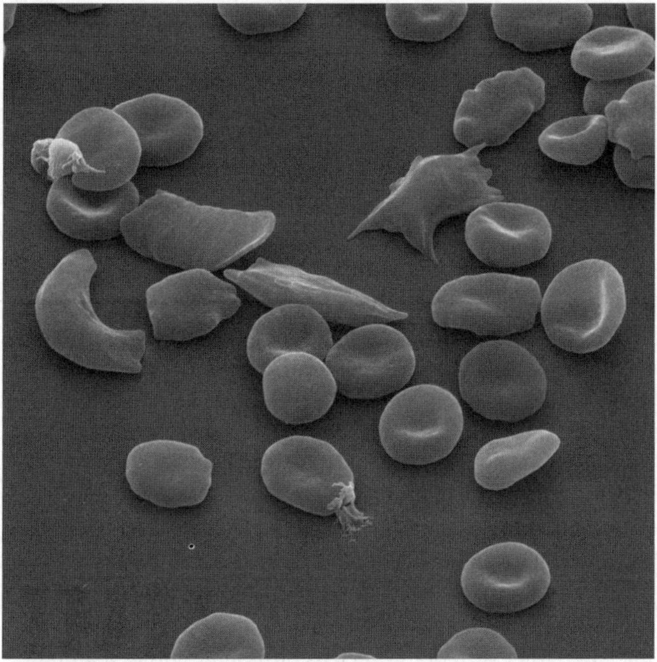

(b) Damaged cells are restricted.

a tenth the diameter of the ovum. Unlike the egg, red cells are not spherical, instead being flexible biconcave disks (Figure 4). This enables them to squeeze through the narrowest of capillaries. They also make up in number what they lack in size. The average human has about five trillion red blood cells per litre of blood or thirty trillion (3×10^{13}) in total, making up a quarter of the total number of cells in the body. The red cell is also known in its Greek translated form, the *erythrocyte*: 'erythro' meaning red and 'cyte' vessel.

What does a red cell consist of? Like all mammalian cells it has an exterior membrane that controls access to an interior solution. The membrane structure is primarily formed by lipids (fat), but proteins bound to this membrane also play a key role. The inside volume of the cell is dominated by the red protein haemoglobin that plays the key role in transporting oxygen from the lungs to the tissue. The haemoglobin is so tightly packed within the cell that it almost forms crystals—indeed in a species such as the rat a semi-crystalline state is observable under the microscope.

An unusual feature of red cells is that they contain no nucleus. Indeed the variety of internal structures—mini organs called 'organelles'—that most human cells possess is completely lacking. It is clear that the red cell has primarily evolved to perform a single function, oxygen transportation. Lacking a nucleus, and the requisite machinery to control the synthesis of new proteins, there is a limited ability for reprogramming or repair. It is almost as if the intention of nature had been to pour all the proteins and other chemicals into a package, release it into the circulation, and let it go. And go it does, each cell making a complete traverse of the body's circulation about once a minute. In its three- to four-month lifetime, this means every cell will do the equivalent of 150,000 laps around the body.

Interestingly, it is only mammalian red blood cells that lack a nucleus. Other vertebrates such as birds and reptiles maintain theirs. Like many deceptively simple questions in evolutionary science there is as yet no definitive answer as to why mammals have lost their red cell nucleus. Perhaps the smaller blood vessel size in mammals demands a more streamlined homogenous shape? Or maybe it just enables more haemoglobin molecules to be packed into the structure, enhancing the amount of oxygen that can be picked up from the lungs.

Oxygen is mainly consumed in tissues by organelles called 'mitochondria', which convert food and oxygen into useful cellular energy. Red cells lack mitochondria; they get their energy by fermenting glucose. This process is similar to that which yeast cells use to make ethanol for beer and wine. But in the red cell, the end product, perhaps fortunately, is lactate rather than ethanol. Having limited energy demands, the red cell can manage with this less efficient oxygen-free process. A prosaic explanation for their lack of mitochondria is that it prevents the loss of any oxygen picked up from the lungs on the cells' journey to the tissues that need it.

The shape of the red cell is both deformable and elastic. In the bloodstream each cell is exposed to large shear forces. Yet, due to the properties of the membrane, they are able to constrict to enter blood vessels smaller in diameter than their normal size, bouncing back to their original shape on exiting the vessel the other side. This ability to safely enter very small openings allows capillaries to be very small. This in turn enables every cell in the body to be close to a capillary. Oxygen consequently only needs to diffuse a short distance from the blood to the surrounding tissue; this is vital as oxygen diffusion outside the bloodstream is very slow. Various pathologies, such as diabetes, peripheral vascular disease, and septic shock disturb this deformability of red blood cells, with deleterious consequences. In sickle cell disease a shape change in the haemoglobin molecule causes a shape change in the red blood cell; during a crisis the cell changes from a biconcave disk to a sickle shape, which can consequently get stuck in capillaries.

Apart from haemoglobin the most well-known proteins on the red cell are those that face the outside of the cell and define the blood type. The cell surface is where communication occurs with the world at large. Although it has limited metabolic needs, like all cells, there are proteins on the red cell surface that regulate the import and export of material and also interact with the environment. Being on the surface they are also sensed by the immune system. Different people will have slightly different versions of these proteins on their surface. During development each person's immune system is trained to recognize the unique fingerprint—or antigen—corresponding to its own proteins. Knowing what is 'self' means that foreign bacterial or viral invaders can be recognized and targeted for destruction. There are a large number of these 'antigens' on the surface of the red cell. So while these surface proteins play a role in normal red cell function, they also define an individual's blood type or blood group.

Over thirty different substances, proteins and carbohydrates, contribute to an individual's blood group. By far the best known are the ABO and Rhesus systems. This is not because the proteins and carbohydrates that comprise these particular blood group types are vitally important for red cell function, but rather because a failure to account for these types during a blood transfusion can have catastrophic consequences.

The ABO blood group is sugar-based (Figure 5). A chain of sugar molecules is bound to the lipid membrane that surrounds the cells. It is not clear what the 'normal' function of this sugar chain is, or indeed whether it has a current function at all or is just a molecular relic of previous evolutionary changes. In the case of blood group A the sugar called 'N-acetylglucosamine' is bound to

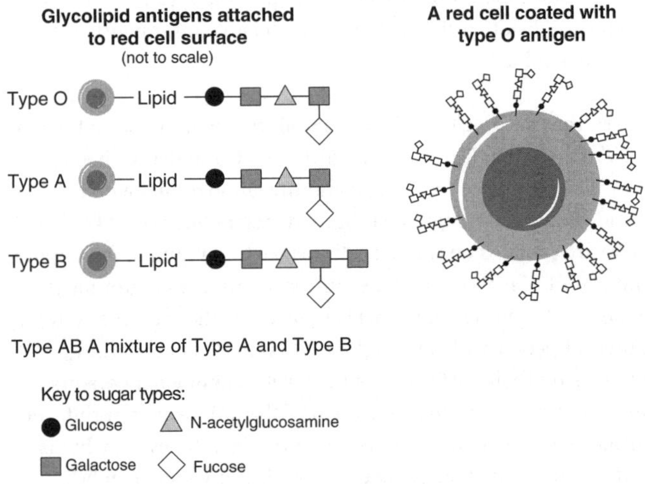

5. Biochemistry of different blood group antigens.

the end of the chain; in the case of blood group B the sugar is D-galactose. Blood Group AB has both N-acetylglucosamine and D-galactose, whereas blood group O has neither. Blood groups are inherited, not because sugars are inherited but because people inherit the DNA for making the protein enzymes that attach or remove the sugars from this chain. Once at the end of the chain, these sugars are strongly 'antigenic'. Foreign blood group antigens will be recognized by the immune system, which will then target the red cell for destruction.

During development the immune system learns to recognize a person's own antigens. So a person born with blood group A will recognize the A sugar as friendly, but will attack the B sugar. A person born with blood group B will recognize the B sugar as friendly, but will attack the A sugar. One with AB will attack neither and one with O will attack both. In general blood is matched to the same blood type. However, blood from an O person can be safely given to anyone (with no sugar antigens this person is a 'universal' donor). An AB person can accept blood from anyone ('universal' recipient) as they recognize both A and B as friendly. Type O blood is therefore more generally useful for transfusion than type A, B, or AB. As all that is needed to convert A and B to O is to remove a sugar, there is commercial and medical interest in devising ways to do this; the most unusual attempt so far being to add an extract from green (unroasted) coffee beans which contains an enzyme that removes the B antigen, and therefore has the potential to convert B type blood to O type.

The prevalence of blood types varies around the world. In Europe types O and A are the most common, while B is more prevalent in North India and Central Asia. In many parts of the world a person's blood group is only of interest if they are donating or receiving blood; people are frequently completely unaware of their own group. However, in Japan and many other East Asian countries, the main ABO blood types are considered by many to be predictive of personality and compatibility with other people;

matchmakers and dating agencies for example pay particular attention to blood type compatibility. Although there is no scientific basis for personality effects, there is some evidence that blood type can affect health more generally. One study in US Caucasians suggested people with blood group AB were 23 per cent more likely than group O to suffer from heart disease, whereas B increased the risk by 11 per cent, and type A by only 5 per cent. On the flip side, patients with AB blood type were found to be 20 per cent less likely to die after heart bypass surgery than those with A, B, or O blood types. Given the minor role that the blood group antigens themselves seem to play in the body, this is almost certainly not a direct effect of the presence or absence of the sugar group antigens on the red cell surface. It far more likely represents a genetic association with other genes that are protective against cardiac disease and are inherited alongside the blood type genes.

The other major blood group is the Rh system, named after the Rhesus monkey, in which it was first discovered. This is protein-based rather than sugar-based. In this case we do know something about its normal role in the body. Rh proteins sit in the lipid membrane of the cell and control the transport of molecules into and out of the cell, most probably carbon dioxide and ammonia. The situation is complex, with over thirty different subgroups relating to subtle differences in the protein structure. However, there is one dominant protein antigen whose presence on the cell surface characterizes an Rh-positive person. As proteins are encoded by DNA, the Rh antigens are genetically inherited. A dangerous situation can arise if a foetus is Rh positive and a mother is Rh negative. This occurs if the baby receives the Rh factor from his/her father. If there is blood mixing during a first pregnancy, some Rh antigen can cross to the mother who will become sensitized and develop antibodies. This does not occur fast enough to damage the first foetus. But it can prove fatal to a second Rh positive foetus as the mother's immune system will recognize the red blood cells as foreign (non-self) and aggressively attack them, destroying the foetal red cells with potentially fatal consequences for the baby. Fortunately, it is possible to largely prevent this by injecting the mother after the first birth with antibodies that kill any foetal cells that have escaped into the mother's circulation; this prevents the mother from mounting her own immune response.

A lack of red blood cells is called 'anaemia'. A lack of iron is the main cause, iron being required to make a functional haemoglobin protein. It is estimated that over one billion people suffer from iron-deficiency anaemia. This can be caused by poor diet or chronic blood loss, of the type associated with parasitic worm infections, ulcers, or gastrointestinal cancers. Anaemia can also be caused by kidney damage or cancer chemotherapy. The former destroys the hormone, erythropoietin, that controls red blood cell development, while the latter damages the bone marrow where red cells are formed.

White cells

If you look through a microscope, hidden among the mass of red cells you will see a few larger colourless cells that are heterogeneous in nature. These are the white blood cells, or leucocytes. They perform many and varied roles in the body, but all are related, in one way or another, to defence against external invaders (pathogens). Unlike the red cells, all white cell subtypes contain nuclei. Some also contain on their surface a set of molecules called the 'major histocompatibility complex' (MHC). In humans, these receptors are also called 'human leucocyte antigens' (HLA). Their role is to recognize fragments of protein from pathogens and trigger the immune response that will ultimately destroy the invaders.

Crudely, white blood cells can be divided into those that attack 'on sight' any foreign material—whether it be a fragment of inanimate material such as a splinter or an invading microorganism—and those that form part of a defence mechanism that recognizes specific biomolecules and marshals a slower, but equally devastating response. In military terms this can be likened to the difference between border defence troops (that shoot on sight any invader) and the mustering of a larger army targeted to the specific threat that has breached these defences. The border defence—or cells of the non-specific (or innate) immune system to give them their proper title—are divided into those that have nuclei with multiple lobed shapes (polymorphonuclear leucocytes or PMN) and those that have a single lobe nucleus (called appropriately 'mononuclear leucocytes' or 'MN'). PMN contain granules inside them and so are sometimes called 'granulocytes'.

Neutrophils are by far the most abundant PMN, making up over half of the total white blood cell count. The primary role of a neutrophil is to engulf a foreign object such as an invading microorganism. In this process, called 'phagocytosis', a part of the neutrophil cell membrane is wrapped around the invader, which is then internalized, forming a 'phagosome'. The invader is now trapped inside a protective membrane, rather like a fly caught inside a spider's web. The membrane separates the internal environment of the phagosome from that of the rest of the neutrophil. However, this membrane is for the protection of the neutrophil, not the invader. For in molecular terms the neutrophil is poised to unleash hell on the invader. The purpose of the intracellular granules now becomes clear. They fuse with the phagosome, in the process depositing a range of destructive enzymes. Proteases break down the invader's proteins in a process analogous to that which happens to food in the gut during digestion: the organism is literally eaten alive. Worse, other granules release destructive enzymes called 'oxidases' and 'peroxidases' which make use of highly reactive iron chemistry. When your car rusts, oxygen oxidizes the iron from the ferrous to the ferric state. Peroxidases use 'superoxidized' ferryl iron that is even more powerful. This ferryl iron is so reactive that compounds containing it are virtually unobtainable by normal chemistry, requiring the special structures that have evolved in proteins to control its reactivity. Peroxidases produce reactive free radicals, hydrogen peroxide and hypochlorous acid. If you look at the contents of a bottle of industrial bleach you will see these same ingredients. Indeed, if you activate neutrophils in a test tube, you can actually smell bleach.

A neutrophil only lasts one or two days following its release into the bloodstream, before itself being phagocytosed by other white blood cells. Like the mayfly, a neutrophil burns brightly for twenty-four hours and then its life is extinguished. Unlike the mayfly, its short life is dedicated towards destruction not reproduction. Congenital defects, certain types of white blood cell cancers (leukaemia), or cancer chemotherapy can cause a shortage of neutrophils (neutropenia), leading to an increased susceptibility to infections. Mutations in one of the oxidases that produces the reactive free radicals have the same deleterious effects, causing chronic granulomatous disease.

Eosinophils and *basophils* are the least abundant PMN cell type, each making up less than 2 per cent of white blood cells. The role of basophils is to respond to tissue injury by triggering an inflammatory response. A closely allied cell, mast cells, do not circulate but instead reside in other parts of the body, where they can trigger inflammation in conditions such as asthma, eczema, rhinitis, and conjunctivitis. When activated, basophils and mast cells degranulate, releasing molecules such as histamine, leukotrienes, and cytokines. Some of these molecules trigger an increase in blood flow causing redness and heat in the damaged site, others sensitize the area to pain. Greater permeability of the blood vessels results in plasma leaking out of the vessels and into the surrounding tissue at an increased rate, causing swelling. We are very familiar with the redness, pain, and swelling caused by an inflammatory insult. This is probably an evolutionary adaptation to prevent overuse of a damaged part of the body but also helps to bring white cells and proteins to the damaged, inflamed area. Removing the inflammatory stimulus quickly reverses these acute effects. Adding ice locally also has an effect, as the lower local temperature dulls the pain and reduces the swelling by decreasing local blood flow. Once restricted to treatment of a defined injury such as a twisted ankle or a 'dead leg', many elite athletes now take an 'ice bath' to aid recovery after matches. Ice does indeed reduce pain and decrease local blood flow. However, the scientific evidence that it is of any benefit in aiding recovery days after the trauma of a strenuous football or tennis match is scant. Indeed, some inflammation is probably beneficial to recovery from injury.

The main function of eosinophils is to tackle invaders too large to be engulfed by neutrophils, such as the multicellular parasitic tapeworms and nematodes. The eosinophil binds to the surface of the worm and expels its granules full of digestive enzymes. In the developing world an increase in eosinophils in the blood is, not surprisingly given their function, most commonly associated with parasitic infections. However, elsewhere eosinophilia is an indicator of a wide range of pathologies, ranging from allergic disorders to autoimmune disorders, and some cancers.

Monocytes are a type of mononuclear leucocyte (MN) making up about 5 per cent of white blood cells. They spend even less time in the circulation than neutrophils, generally less than ten hours, but their time in the blood circulation does not end in death. Instead, they are converted into a cell called a 'macrophage', which either becomes fixed in a tissue or moves slowly around the body in an amoeboid fashion. Their role is similar to the neutrophil, acting as a recycling system and phagocytosing foreign material. They also remove dead and dying cells from the circulation; the ultimate fate of both the red blood cell and the neutrophil is to be engulfed by a macrophage. An excess of monocytes in a blood count (monocytosis) is an indicator of chronic inflammation; more tests would be needed to determine whether the cause was external (e.g. bacteria or viral infection) or internal (e.g. autoimmune disease or some types of cancer).

Lymphocytes (also a type of MN) are the second largest population of white blood cells, making up approximately 30 per cent of the total. They come in two types, large granular lymphocytes and small lymphocytes. Large granular lymphocytes come in a variety of types, but the most significant are probably the wonderfully named 'Natural Killer' (or NK) cells. NK cells do not recognize specific types of invaders; like neutrophils and eosinophils, they are part of the non-specific innate immune system. They target cells already infected by a virus. NKs kill these cells, not by phagocytosis, but instead by releasing toxic enzymes inside them (called 'granzymes'). Granzymes kill the host cell and stop the virus replicating. NKs are also able to kill certain types of cancer cells, possibly preventing the spread of the disease.

Small lymphocytes are probably the most interesting and well-studied of the white blood cells, as they give the immune system its specificity. These cells give us the ability to respond to specific molecules and organisms and, more importantly, to remember that response so that we become immune to future attacks. This process is called 'immunity' and is the basis for all vaccination programmes. There are two types of cells in this acquired, or adaptive, immune system: *B lymphocytes* and *T lymphocytes*. The B cells produce specific proteins called 'antibodies'; these recognize an invading cell and target it for destruction by other cells. They are the biological equivalents of laser 'painting' a military target so that it can be more accurately targeted by a bomb. T cells also recognize specific alien molecules but have the ability to do the destruction themselves, acting as judge, jury, and executioner. Because they have to recognize a huge variety of targets there are very many different B lymphocytes and T lymphocytes in the blood circulation at any one time. They are also the most long-lived of white blood cells, with the half-life of an individual cell being as long as five to six weeks.

An increase in the number of lymphocytes in a blood test is most commonly associated with a viral infection. The most common form of adult leukaemia (chronic lymphoid leukaemia) is also associated with overproduction of B lymphocytes. In contrast in the most common childhood leukaemia (acute lymphoblastic leukaemia), there is an overproduction of immature lymphocytes called 'lymphoblasts'. As opposed to the controlled response to infection, in these cancers the uncontrolled production of these white cells is at the expense of other useful cell types, such as red cells and platelets.

Platelets and blood clotting

Platelets are far more numerous than white blood cells, compromising 5–10 per cent of the number of red blood cells. However, they are some of the smallest cells in the body and, like the red cell, contain no nucleus. They are unique to mammalian blood and have only one function—the prevention of excess bleeding. If the lining of a blood vessel is damaged, proteins such as collagen become exposed. Circulating proteins bind to the collagen. This protein complex is recognized by platelets, which gather at the scene of the wound. The platelets can then bind to each other, forming a physical barrier that is able to plug a small hole.

A complex series of enzymatic reactions, called the 'coagulation cascade', also ensues (Figure 6). The final stage of this cascade is the conversion of the circulating protein fibrinogen to fibrin by the activated enzyme, thrombin. Fibrinogen is a soluble protein, but fibrin—as its name suggests—forms long strands of insoluble fibres; these cross-link together and bind to the platelets at the wound site, forming the blood clot that prevents further bleeding. Although not a strict analogy, we are all familiar with other protein structural changes that can convert liquid into solid; this happens for example when we boil an egg (when the protein in the egg, called 'albumin', changes its structure).

Blood coagulation is a target for predatory organisms. In its more benign form animals that eat blood such as leeches, vampire bats,

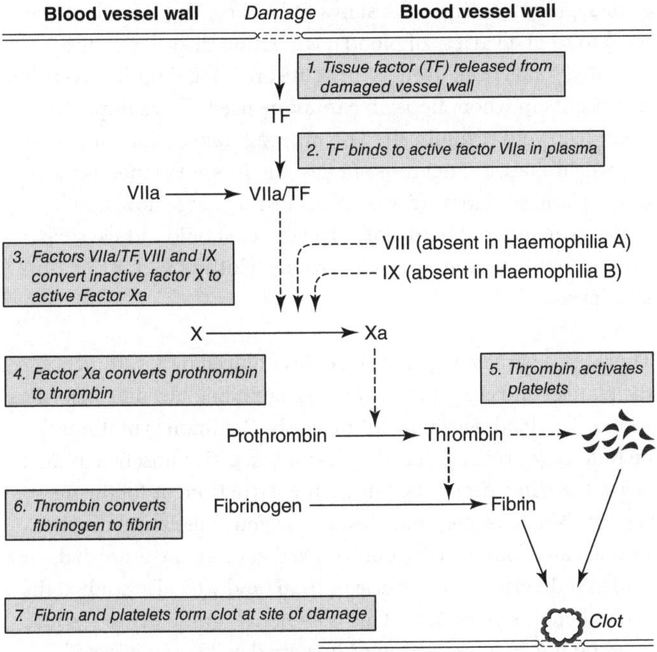

6. The coagulation cascade. This simplified scheme illustrates how the lack of protein factors VIII or IX prevent clot formation and cause the bleeding disorder haemophilia.

and mosquitos need to ensure a continuous supply of blood from the injection site and therefore inject compounds that increase blood flow and act as anticoagulants. These organisms need to keep their victims alive and, ideally, unaware of their presence. Venomous snakes are not so benign to their victims. Many poisons in snake venom dramatically affect blood coagulation. Some snakes use anticoagulant venom resulting in the victim bleeding to death; others use procoagulants to induce fatal blood clots.

Medicine has been able to make good use of both anticoagulants and procoagulants found in nature. For example, hirudin is an anticoagulant found in the saliva of leeches. Historically it was used to treat a variety of blood coagulation disorders; more recently, it has been used as an acute anticoagulant intervention in patients in whom heparin cannot be used, for example to treat deep vein thrombosis. The procoagulant venom of one of the world's most dangerous snakes, the Russell's viper, is used in the standard laboratory Stypven test to gauge how well a patient's blood is able to clot. The venom should induce a clot rapidly, but if a patient is deficient in a clotting factor this time is delayed.

There are a variety of genetic diseases induced by a dysfunction in the platelet and coagulation systems, including bleeding disorders where the blood does not clot properly. Common symptoms include easy bruising, bleeding gums, excessive nosebleeds, and heavy bleeding after cuts, during menstruation, or following surgery. The most common disorder is Von Willebrand disease. This is named after Erik Adolf von Willebrand, the Finnish doctor who first described the disease in 1926 (and who also studied the health benefits of saunas). This is a relatively mild disease; some cases do not require treatment in everyday life, but affected patients need to be carefully managed to reduce bleeding during surgery. This disease is caused by a lack of the von Willebrand factor, a large protein that interacts with a number of clotting factors in the coagulation cascade. One of these is factor VIII, the lack of which is the cause of the most famous bleeding disorder—haemophilia A. The gene for factor VIII can be found on the X chromosome, and is therefore a sex-linked disease. It is recessive; as long as you have one good copy of the gene you remain largely unaffected. Therefore women, who have two X chromosomes, can pass the disease onto their sons but are not themselves affected by the disease except for the very rare circumstance where both X chromosomes carry the defective gene. On the other hand, males, who have one X and one Y chromosome, will be affected if their one X chromosome has the defective gene.

A rarer form of haemophilia, haemophilia B, is caused by the lack of blood clotting factor IX, rather than VIII. This rare disease has great historical significance, at least for those interested in the recent history of European royalty. Recent blood tests of the bones of the Russian Romanov family suggest that Queen Victoria carried this disease, probably via a spontaneous mutation in one of her X chromosomes. How did the disease travel from the queen of Britain to Russia (Figure 7)? One of Queen Victoria's four sons, Prince Leopold, suffered from the disease, dying from blood loss after he slipped and fell. Of her five daughters, at least two seem to have carried the disease, Alice and Beatrice. They married Grand Duke Louis IV (of Hesse and by Rhine) and Prince Henry of Battenberg, respectively. Alice had nine children and Beatrice four; by the custom of the day these children married royalty across Europe, spreading Queen Victoria's bleeding mutation far and wide (and temporarily labelling haemophilia as the 'royal disease').

The fate of Alice's daughter Princess Alix is perhaps the most interesting. Alix received an offer of marriage from her first cousin, Albert, the eldest son of the man who would later become Britain's King Edward VII. But Alix refused the offer; the British monarchy consequently had a lucky escape from the re-introduction of Queen Victoria's mutant gene. However, Britain's 'loss' was Russia's 'gain', as Alix ended up marrying Tsar Nicholas II. Their only son, the Tsarevich Alexei, suffered from haemophilia. Alix, now Empress Alexandra, relied on the mystic monk Rasputin to heal her son during his many bleeding crises. What Rasputin actually did is disputed. However, it seems clear that he exuded a calming effect on the young boy and insisted that doctors should stay well away. This itself may have been good advice: there was no known cure at the time. The new wonder drug of the time—aspirin—is itself an anticoagulant, so doing nothing was probably the best option. However, Rasputin's increased influence on the empress was enabled by his 'success' as a spiritual healer.

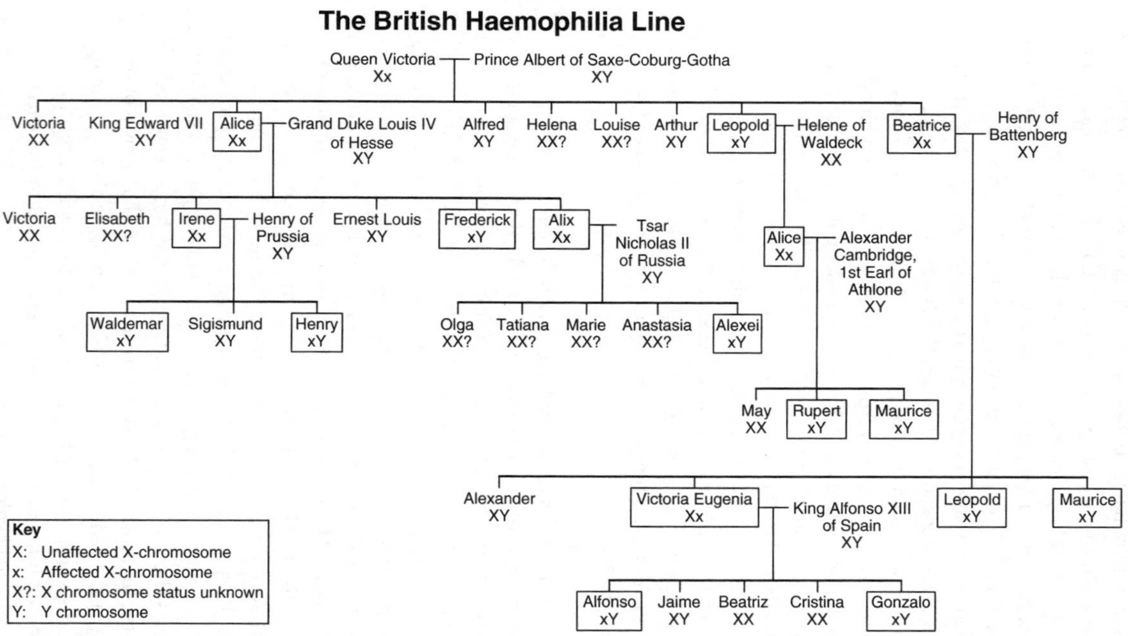

7. Tracing the path of Queen Victoria's haemophilia B gene through European royalty. Royals enclosed in boxes are either carriers (female) or sufferers (male).

In more recent times haemophiliacs and patients with Von Willebrand disease have been successfully treated with concentrated preparations of blood clotting factors prepared from donated blood. However, in the 1980s and 1990s these were contaminated with the HIV/AIDS and hepatitis viruses—making the treatment worse than the disease in a worrying echo of Rasputin's plea against medical interference. However, new tests, and the production of synthetic coagulation factors, have now removed this risk.

Plasma

Blood has to flow freely. Therefore, the red cells, white cells, and platelets are all suspended in a watery solution called 'plasma'. But plasma is more than just water. In fact if it were only water all the cells would burst. Plasma has to have a very similar concentration of molecules and ions as the cells. This is because cells are permeable to water. So if the concentration of dissolved substances in the plasma was significantly higher than that in the cells, water would flow from the cells to the plasma in an attempt to equalize this gradient by diluting the plasma; this would result in cell shrinkage. Even worse, if the concentration in the plasma was lower than in the cells, water would flow into the cells from the plasma, and the resulting pressure increase would burst the cells, releasing all their contents into the plasma in the process.

Ions are elements that have become charged by gaining or losing an electron. An example is common salt, which is made up of positively charged sodium ions and negatively charged chloride ions. A solution that has the same concentration of ions as the cells they surround is called 'isotonic'. To prevent cell shrinkage or bursting, the body has mechanisms to maintain the plasma in an isotonic state. Sports drink manufacturers have latched onto this idea and 'isotonic' sports drinks are heavily marketed. However, there is nothing magic in the formulation and they can also be made easily, and more cheaply, at home by adding a quarter of a teaspoon of sodium chloride (common salt) to a litre of water or a flavoured squash or cordial drink. During sport, drinking an isotonic fluid to replace the body's salt levels is really only necessary when exercising intensely for durations of over an hour.

Plasma contains much more than just the ions required to prevent cells bursting or shrinking. It also contains key components designed to assist in cellular function. The protein clotting factors that are part of the coagulation cascade are always present in low concentrations, ready to be activated by platelets and other factors when necessary to form a clot. Low levels of antibodies, produced by the lymphocytes, circulate, primed to trigger the specific immune defence system. In addition to antibodies, the plasma contains C-reactive proteins, Mannose-binding lectin and complement proteins that function as 'opsonins'; this term derives from the Greek *opsōneîn*, 'to prepare for eating', and reflects their role in targeting foreign molecules for digestion and destruction by the body's defences.

A host of other proteins perform roles independent of oxygen delivery or immune defence. By far the most abundant protein in serum is albumin. In the confined capillaries hydrostatic pressure tends to push water out of the plasma. However, the albumin molecule is too large in size to cross the walls of small capillaries. This creates a pressure (called 'colloid osmotic pressure' or 'oncotic pressure') that pulls fluid back into the capillaries from the surrounding cells until the local protein concentration is equalized. This colloid osmotic pressure (pulling water in) therefore balances the hydrostatic pressure (pushing water out). However, in clinical conditions, such as proteinuria, albumin is filtered out of the plasma via the kidneys and ends up in the urine; the resulting low plasma albumin level allows fluid to leave the capillaries and build up in the surrounding tissues, causing oedema (or swelling). Patients in hospitals are frequently put on intravenous drips. The fluid in such drips needs to be balanced with the ions and proteins in blood. As a first response, isotonic ('normal') saline (sodium chloride) or a similar solution is used. If there is a concern about maintaining the colloid osmotic pressure, a protein solution can be used instead. This is sometimes albumin itself, or sometimes a synthetic colloid such as gelatin. Neither solution can deliver oxygen, so if there has been significant blood loss a red cell transfusion will be needed as well.

Blood is the transport infrastructure for any molecule that needs to be moved around the body. Some, such as the water-soluble fuel glucose, and small hormones like insulin, dissolve freely in the plasma. Others that are less soluble hitch a ride on proteins; albumin itself binds fat-soluble molecules such as steroid hormones and the fuel source, fatty acids. Dangerous reactive molecules, such as iron, are also bound to proteins, in this case transferrin. Transferrin performs the dual role of transporting iron around the body and limiting the amount of reactive free iron in the plasma. The latter has two beneficial effects. In its free form iron can be quite dangerous and initiate free radical chemistry (rather like that of the white blood cell peroxidases). However, it is also an important mineral used by pathogenic microorganisms. So transferrin both keeps iron safe from damaging the body and starves invading organisms of a requisite for their growth.

Chapter 3
Fighting disease

Vaccination

In Chapter 2, we learnt that our white blood cells are a key component of the immune system that defends us from bacterial, parasite, and viral attack. However, an understanding of how the immune system works is much more complicated—and more interesting—than the simple description of cell function given in that chapter.

In evolutionary terms the immune system has its roots in the recognition, and destruction, of foreign bodies. It is not hard to see how natural selection would favour an ability to recognize foreign (non-self) biological molecules. For the earliest primitive single celled organisms this would be as much about recognizing a food supply as defence against an attack. At school we might look down the microscope at a slide of a single cell amoeba feeding by engulfing its prey. This same process, 'phagocytosis', is used when macrophages or the white blood cell neutrophils attack invading bacteria.

The basic idea—recognize intruder and destroy immediately—is fundamental to the defence systems of all organisms from fungi to plants and mammals. A more complicated system, adaptive immunity, evolved in animals with backbones—the vertebrates.

This relies on immunological memory, a unique property of the white blood cell B and T lymphocytes. Once bitten twice shy. Or rather once bitten twice attack aggressively and kill all invaders.

The immense power of this adaptive response was revealed by vaccination. The standard story is well known with Edward Jenner as its hero. Jenner, the sixth son of an English country vicar, was orphaned at age 5. Growing up in Berkeley in Gloucestershire, Jenner was a part time flute player and poet, but full time physician. He was also fascinated by natural history and found time to do scientific research in his spare time. Indeed his research on how baby cuckoos survived by throwing the eggs of hedge sparrows out of the nest won him a prestigious fellowship of the Royal Society.

Although Jenner is credited as the 'inventor' of vaccination, as is often the case with science, the story is not quite so clear. Before Jenner it was already known that inoculation with matter from smallpox pustules (variolation) could provide immunity from the disease. Nowadays we would call this an attempt at vaccination with a live, though attenuated (weakened), virus. The first recorded use was by the Chinese in the 15th century; they chose those suffering from mild smallpox as donors, grinding up their pustules and blowing the powdered scabs up the nostrils of the patient. In the Arabic world there was a trade in the selling of pustules for variolation known as *Tishteree el Jidderi*, or 'buying the smallpox'. However, the medicine was often as bad as the disease, with the added problem that variolation did nothing to stop the spread of the virus itself. The Chinese originators were well aware of this fact for, following variolation, those inoculated were treated as if they had the full disease and kept in isolation until their scabs cleared.

Variolation spread to the European world at the beginning of the 18th century, and from there to the Americas; George Washington ordered compulsory variolation for his revolutionary Continental

Army in 1775. The basic method was adapted, with ongoing attempts at improving its safety. Jenner originally used the methods of Robert Sutton. At first kept secret, to ensure maximum profit for Sutton's clinics, the method was later revealed as an English version of the Chinese method—again using only mild donors but introducing the dose via a minor scratch rather than nasally. However, as in China, the recipients became infectious. So while variolation did indeed provide some defence for the recipient, it could be argued that it led to a greater spread of the disease itself with an enhanced population of relatively healthy disease carriers walking around the English towns and countryside.

The principle of variolation was correct: inject people with a mild version of an infectious disease so that they are later protected against the full version. But the agent was wrong. Nowadays most vaccinations are not live viruses at all, but isolated chemical components of the virus. That way there is no risk of spreading the disease. Jenner needed a genuinely safe version of smallpox. He found it when he noted that some people had no reaction to variolation, producing no rash at all. These people had previously contracted cowpox, a disease related to smallpox but that infected cattle not humans. In fact, it was relatively common knowledge at the time that animal poxes protected against later infection with smallpox. The British army, for example, had noticed that cavalrymen, whose horses were hosts to a milder version of smallpox, were less susceptible to smallpox than infantry.

While many suspected the link from animal poxes to human protection against smallpox, Jenner had the intellectual drive and daring to follow it to its natural conclusion. In 1796 he inoculated James Phipps, an 8-year-old boy, with material from a young maid called Sarah Nelmes, who was suffering with cowpox. Phipps contracted cowpox and then Jenner, with his parent's consent, inoculated the boy with smallpox. The smallpox had no effect and Jenner's place in history as the father of vaccination was assured.

Jenner was not alone in being interested in cowpox inoculation as a cure for smallpox. During the previous twenty years, at least six people were credited with performing such procedures before Jenner. These included Jobst Bose from Göttingen in Germany and Benjamin Jesty, a farmer from Dorset, England. Jesty even injected his wife and two children during an epidemic of smallpox. Some of these methods were indeed published well before Jenner's 'discovery'. Dr John Fewster from Gloucester reported on 'Cow pox and its ability to prevent smallpox' at a meeting of the Royal Society of Medicine in 1765, but did not publish in print. Peter Plett, a teacher in Germany, vaccinated three children with cowpox lymph to protect them against smallpox. In 1790 and 1791 he reported this success to the University of Kiel, but they favoured the variolation technique and ignored him.

So why was Jenner especially credited with the discovery? At least two reasons stand out. First on scientific, if perhaps not ethical grounds, he did the key experiment. Inoculating an uninfected child first with cowpox and then smallpox proved the protective effect of the vaccination. Jenner was also a key figure in publicizing and promoting research about vaccination. However, his first attempt to publish his findings in a paper to the Royal Society was rejected. Undaunted he wrote an influential, short, self-published book, called *An Inquiry Into the Cause and Effects of the Variolae Vaccina*. It is perhaps worth noting, however, that for today's scientific community self-publishing a paper that has been rejected by peer review would be the ultimate admission of quackery!

Jenner also championed the cause of vaccination and promoted its use throughout Britain; and it was Jenner who termed the word 'vaccination' for the process of inoculation and 'virus' for the agent that caused cowpox and smallpox. However, even this term was not unique to Jenner—the word 'virus' was first used in relation to an infectious agent in 1728 with reference to venereal disease.

As Francis Galton famously said, 'In science credit goes to the man who convinces the world, not the man to whom the idea first occurs'. Nonetheless, even the most revisionist of vaccination historians still place Jenner as first among equals. This seems appropriate for a man who, unlike Robert Sutton, did not seek to profit from his invention, but instead championed its widespread introduction against considerable opposition.

The cellular immune system

Vaccination is the ultimate demonstration of the adaptive immune system, the body learning to defend itself against future attack. But at the start of the 19th century there was no theoretical underpinning of why vaccination worked. Indeed the causative agents of infectious diseases in general were not widely known. In 1546 the Italian physician scholar and atomist, Girolamo Fracastoro, published his book *On Contagion, Contagious Diseases and Their Cure*, possibly the first place where it was suggested that small particles, invisible to the naked eye, could transmit infectious diseases. But this idea was not favoured. Instead the alternative 'miasma' theory of infection held sway right up until, and even past, the time of Jenner's vaccination work. This was proposed in the 2nd century by Galen. Rotting organic material released a poisonous vapour—called 'miasma'; it was exposure to this vapour that caused the disease. Crucially, the miasma could not pass from individual to individual; people were not infected, the stagnant environment was the infectious agent. Interestingly the theory that a 'stagnant environment' causes disease, while erroneous, contains a kernel of truth. Improving the local environment, including advances in public health and sanitation, has been at least as important as the direct assault on microorganisms in countering infectious diseases.

The discovery of cells by the English physicist Robert Hooke in 1665 changed our view of biological material. But the real breakthrough in cellular immunology came when the Italian entomologist Agostino Bassi discovered in 1835 that muscardine, an infectious disease of domestic silkworms, was caused by a very small parasite. Muscardine was literally a plague on the highly lucrative 19th-century Italian silk industry.

Beginning in 1807, Bassi started a thirty-year study of this problem. The first eight years were 'wasted' as he tried to 'prove' two current theories—spontaneous formation of the disease either to an adverse environment or the generation of hyperacidity in the tissues. However, well-controlled experiments are never failures. Bassi believed passionately that facts should inform judgements, rather than the reverse. He therefore looked for new facts that might explain the disease. He noted that the infection correlated with a white efflorescence that gathered on the dead silkworm. When injected into live animals, this material killed and mummified the worms, producing spores in the process. He demonstrated that the infectious agent was organic and living. Under the microscope it had the appearance of a fungus. Bassi used this knowledge to develop a whole range of methods to prevent the disease. He went on to suggest that infectious agents were the cause of human diseases such as smallpox, typhus, rabies, gonorrhoea, syphilis, and cholera. Consequently he strongly advocated sterilizing needles used for vaccination.

Muscardine was the first documented example of a microorganism causing an infectious disease. Later in the 19th century Louis Pasteur, brilliantly expanding on the work of the German physician scientists Robert Koch and Friedrich Henle, formally expounded the germ theory of human disease. The miasma was dead and the microorganism was firmly established as the chief villain.

Pasteur knew how to kill microorganisms. In his Paris laboratory, he developed the heating process known today as 'pasteurization', where solutions such as wine or beer are heated to 50–60°C for a brief time to decrease the activity of microbes. Pasteur was also able to weaken microorganisms in his laboratory by exposing them to oxygen, chemicals, or dehydration. These attenuated organisms could then be used safely for vaccination. This removed the requirement to hunt for a weaker version of the infectious organism in nature, as was the case with smallpox/cowpox. Pasteur, his collaborators and peers were able to develop new vaccines for anthrax, cholera, and rabies. The golden age of vaccination had begun.

But it was still a mystery how the body defended itself against these micro invaders. In the words of Professor the Count K. A. H. Mörner, rector of the Royal Caroline Institute (now the Karolinska Institute in Stockholm), on 10 December 1908:

> Great though the practical importance of Jenner's discovery was, it did not advance the development of the study of immunity in respect of other diseases or permit of any deep penetration into the problem of immunity generally.

This speech was delivered at the presentation ceremony for the Nobel Prize in Physiology and Medicine in 1908 to the Russian/Ukrainian scientist, Élie Metchnikoff. Metchnikoff had visited Pasteur in 1888 to ask him for some advice on his rabies vaccinations. Pasteur was so impressed that he offered him a job there and then, and Metchnikoff spent the remaining twenty-eight years of his life in Paris. Metchnikoff was by all accounts a difficult scientist to get on with. He was frequently angry and chronically depressed. His mother dissuaded him from a medical career as she felt he was too sensitive to deal with the suffering of patients. He attempted suicide at least twice: the first time he was too eager and was saved by the emetic properties of the large vial of morphine he swallowed; the second time he inoculated himself with a bacterium that caused a relapsing fever. 'Failing' again, he turned his suicide into a scientific study, by seeing if his now infected blood could transmit the disease further.

Yet Pasteur had recognized Metchnikoff's genius and could cope with his faults. What Metchnikoff had seen was the link between digestion and the immune system. He was studying comparative embryology by looking at the development of starfish larvae; these had the advantage of being transparent and thus made for easy observation. When observing digestion in these larvae, he was surprised that the red dye (carmine) he added was engulfed by cells, even though it was not a nutrient. His 'Eureka' moment came one morning in Italy in 1882:

> One day when the whole family had gone to a circus to see some extraordinary performing apes, I remained alone with my microscope, observing the life in the mobile cells of a transparent star-fish larva, when a new thought suddenly flashed across my brain. It struck me that similar cells might serve in the defence of the organism against intruders. Feeling that there was in this something of surpassing interest, I felt so excited that I began striding up and down the room and even went to the seashore in order to collect my thoughts.
>
> I said to myself that, if my supposition was true, a splinter introduced into the body of a starfish larva, devoid of blood vessels or of a nervous system, should soon be surrounded by mobile cells as is to be observed in a man who runs a splinter into his finger. This was no sooner said than done. (O. Metchnikoff, *Life of Elie Metchnikoff*, Boston: Houghton Mifflin Co., 1921)

Injecting rose thorns under the skin of the larvae led, after a sleepless night, to the desired result. The thorn was surrounded and engulfed by these motile cells. This one observation—followed up by twenty-five more years of careful study and experiment—led to the phagocytic theory of immune defence. The mechanisms of cellular attack during digestion are the same as those used by the body to defend against attack. Just as the starfish motile cells attacked the thorn, so a wood splinter is attacked by our white blood cells, causing swelling at the site of injury.

Cells or molecules?

Metchnikoff knew that cells were not the sole mediators of the immune system. For Pasteur himself had developed antitoxins, which were effective against disease but were not cellular. This acellular component of the immune system—humoral immunity—was in large part developed by another gentleman who was listening to Count Mörner's speech in Stockholm. This man was Paul Ehrlich, who shared the 1908 Nobel Prize with Metchnikoff. Ehrlich was a German chemist who has a good claim to be the founder of the modern pharmaceutical industry, having developed the chemical concept of a 'magic bullet', a molecule that specifically attacks the desired target (he invented the first synthetic chemical drug, the antisyphilis agent Arsphenamine). Ehrlich was a collaborator of Emil von Behring. Behring was the first to show that injecting a toxin produced from the diphtheria bacterium into an animal resulted in the animal's blood developing protection to the disease. Therefore Behring surmised that injecting the serum from that animal into a human has the potential to cure that disease. Antisera are still used today, though primarily as treatments for the bites of venomous animals such as snakes and spiders. Dilute venom is injected into the animal and the resulting serum is injected into the patient as antivenom. When no other treatment is available, such as when patients are infected with the Ebola virus, serum from a human survivor is sometimes tried as a therapy.

Behring won the first ever Nobel Prize in Physiology or Medicine in 1901. But it was Ehrlich who developed the theoretical underpinning for this work, and hence its relevance to the immune system. Ehrlich proposed his 'side chain' theory, according to which each toxin interacted with specific chemical side chains pre-existing in the body. Ehrlich knew from his chemistry background the wide variety of organic molecules that could be produced. It was therefore a natural leap of thought to imagine that the blood contained a variety of pre-existing organic side chains that could interact with the toxins, one for each toxin. Nowadays we would call these 'side chains' antibodies, and the specificity of an antibody for a foreign molecule (or antigen) is the basis of modern immunology.

Cells *and* molecules

Following the joint award of the 1908 Nobel Prize there was a heated debate between the supporters of the two great scientists, Ehrlich and Metchnikoff. Were the body's defences based on cells (Metchnikoff) or on chemicals (Ehrlich)? In fact both answers were true. The Nobel Committee's prescience in awarding a shared prize in 1908 was revealed later in the 20th century when it was discovered that the white blood cells (lymphocytes) that recognize the invading microorganisms and prepare them for phagocytosis are coated with versions of the same antibody-like molecules that swim freely in the plasma solution. The specificity of the cellular (lymphocyte) and humoral (antibody) systems is therefore founded on the same chemistry—that of the family of proteins called 'immunoglobulins'.

Immunoglobulin molecules provide the key both to how the body creates the variety of molecules needed to protect against the different invaders experienced over a lifetime, and to how vaccination against a disease protects against future infection. Immunoglobulins are produced by B lymphocytes and either remain bound on the surface of the cell (as part of the B cell receptor) or circulate free in the plasma (as antibodies). Whatever their location, their purpose is the same—to bind to and capture foreign molecules (antigens). The antigen can either be part of an isolated foreign chemical in the plasma or part of the surface of an invading cell. The immunoglobulin then 'presents' the antigen to its target (Figure 8). This can either be phagocytosing cells (such as neutrophils) or other proteins (such as the complement cascade, a collection of plasma proteins that form a 'membrane attack complex' to kill the invading cell).

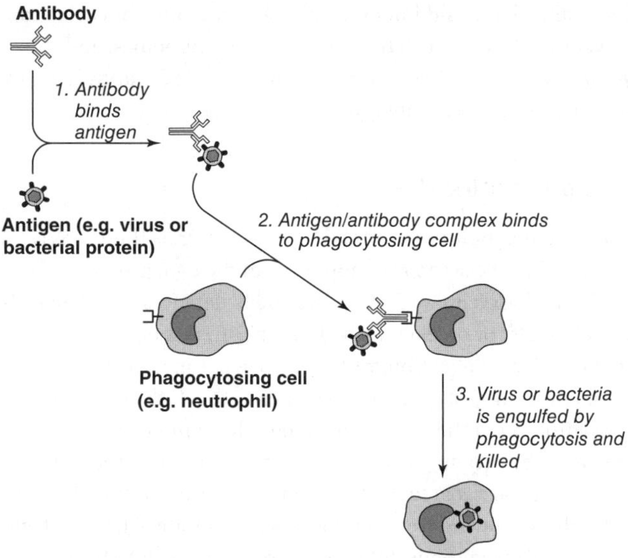

8. How an antibody targets a foreign antigen for destruction.

To perform the twin role of binding the antigen and the phagocytosing cell, immunoglobulins need to have two distinct parts to their structure—one that recognizes the foreign antigen and one that can be recognized—and destroyed—by the host defence system. The host defence system does not vary; a specific type of immunoglobulin will be recognized by one of the relatively few types of immune cells or proteins. Therefore this part of the immunoglobulin structure is not variable. But the nature of the foreign antigen will vary greatly; so the antigen-recognizing part of the structure must be highly variable. It is this that leads to the great variety of immunoglobulins.

The structure of an antibody is illustrated in Figure 9. Antibodies comprise light and heavy protein chains, each of which is further subdivided into constant and variable regions. Constant regions enable interaction with the molecules of the cellular and humoral

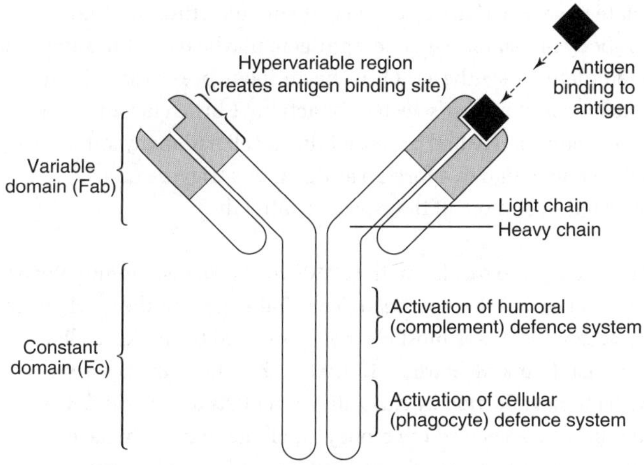

9. Antibody (immunoglobulin) structure.

immune defence systems. Variable regions are specific for the variety of foreign antigens, the antigen binding site itself being especially (hyper)variable. In the hypervariable region about 10^{12} or a trillion different molecules are theoretically possible. Therefore within the blood there is an army of potential binding sites that can recognize and bind to almost any conceivable chemical structure. Such variety is why the body is able to adapt and kill even organisms it has never encountered before. Indeed the ability to make an immunoglobulin recognize almost any structure has resulted in antibody binding assays being used historically in diagnostic tests ranging from pregnancy to drugs testing.

So the variety is present theoretically. But as a consequence, at any one time, there is unlikely to be a large amount of a specific immunoglobulin. Probably only about thirty cells in the entire body exist that can attack any specific invader. Yet the invader will come *en masse* with millions of cells. Immediate action is required to increase the specific immunoglobulin targeted to the attack. How does the body know what to produce and how does this relate to vaccination? Does the body manufacture each new antibody in response to a new antigen, maybe using the antigen as a template for synthesis? Or is the antibody pre-existing in the plasma and then just selected for action? Ehrlich favoured the latter solution. He had proposed that a cell had many antibodies. When one bound to a foreign antigen, this triggered the production of more of that specific antibody.

This idea was expanded in the 1950s by the Danish immunologist Niels Jerne and the American David Talmage. But the mechanism we accept today was most clearly formulated by the Australian scientist, Frank Macfarlane Burnet in the 1950s. Burnet is viewed with special affection by Australian scientists as, surprisingly for the time, he eschewed the money and fame that might have followed a move to Britain or America, and spent the vast majority of his time working in Melbourne. His seminal paper on the 'clonal theory of antibody production' was even published in a rather obscure local journal—the *Australian Journal of Science*—rather than the more prestigious international vehicles. However, combined with his follow up 1959 book—*The Clonal Selection Theory of Acquired Immunity*—his ideas quickly found favour, revolutionizing the field of adaptive immunity.

Burnet's theory was that each of the many billions of B lymphocyte cells has only one immunoglobulin on its surface that recognizes just one kind of antigen shape. When a foreign antigen arrives it is bound to that, and only that, one cell. However, the binding triggers cell division. Billions and billions of clones are made of that cell. These cells also recognize the invading antigen, but more importantly they secrete into the plasma, and other bodily fluids, large numbers of antibodies that can bind to the invading antigen. These target the invader for destruction. While most of the clone cells die after a few weeks, a small fraction become long lived 'memory cells'. These lie dormant until the next time an invader appears. The second response, bolstered by the presence of these memory cells, is more immediate and more extreme. So we finally have an explanation for Jenner's vaccination. The body responds to the antigen of the non-lethal cowpox virus by producing clones of B lymphocytes that can recognize the virus particles. These, and the antibodies they secrete, eventually kill all the cowpox and the patient recovers. However, the memory B lymphocytes that remain recognize *both* cowpox and smallpox (as the viruses are so similar). So when the potentially lethal smallpox arrives, the immune system is prepared. The memory cells recognize the virus antigen, the appropriate B cells clone themselves, and a deluge of antibodies 'paint' the surface of the virus and target it for destruction. Later, T lymphocytes were also shown to possess a similar memory function.

Ground-breaking though it was, Burnet's clonal selection theory was not mentioned in the award of his Nobel Prize in 1960. Instead he was honoured for his work on the discovery of 'acquired immunological tolerance'. This answered the key remaining question of immunology. If we have all these antibodies coursing through our blood that can recognize and destroy any molecule, why does the body not self-destruct?

The immune system is not fully developed in a foetus. All the antibodies are present, but they do not initiate the destruction of foreign molecules. In effect the immunological gun is loaded, but not fired. Burnet therefore reasoned that the immune response system must begin naïve and be acquired during development. It is at this crucial development stage that the body becomes aware of what is self. Anything that antibodies bind to at this stage is noted and considered safe for life. Only after this imprinting stage is complete is it safe to load the gun and fire up the full immune system.

An analogy can be drawn with baby ducks that follow the first moving thing they see. Usually this is their mother, but in the famous animal behaviour studies of Konrad Lorenz, they can be trained to follow a human if that is their first encounter. Burnet's co-recipient of the Nobel Prize, Sir Peter Medawar, was able to demonstrate this effect by 'imprinting' immunological tolerance to foreign molecules as long as they were introduced at the foetal or neonatal stage. These molecules would never trigger a subsequent immune response. Using this method, organs could be successfully transplanted from mice not genetically related to the recipient. In Burnet's words, they had solved the 'central problem in immunology'.

With the 1960 award of the Nobel Prize to Burnet and Medawar, it is indeed possible to claim that the fundamental roles of the white blood cells had become clear. All that remained was to put the pieces together and fill out the detail. But research did not end there. Just as Watson and Crick's discovery of the structure of DNA led to our modern genetic age, so Burnet and Medawar's work led to an explosion of understanding of the cellular and molecular details of our immune system.

One such breakthrough required the skills of both immunology and DNA biology. With an increased understanding of DNA, the genome and proteins, it became clear there was a real problem at the molecular heart of immunology. We could face tens of millions of different foreign molecules over our lifetime. Yet immunoglobulins are proteins. They are encoded by pieces of DNA (genes). The human body has fewer than 30,000 genes that can code for different proteins. This is nowhere near the hundred million that are likely to be needed for the immune system, even if all the proteins in the human body were antibodies. The enigma was solved by the Japanese scientist Susumu Tonegawa. In the winter of 1971, he found himself 'surrounded by immunologists' in the Basel Institute for Immunology in Switzerland. But, crucially, Tonegawa had been trained in the new techniques of molecular biology at the Salk Institute in California and was comfortable with cloning and rearranging pieces of DNA. Bringing these new skills into the field of immunology gave him unique insights.

At the time it was generally thought that each cell had the same complement of DNA. What distinguished a kidney cell from a liver cell would be how that DNA was converted into proteins—with some genes turned on and some turned off. Tonegawa postulated, and then proved, that this was not the case for the B lymphocytes that produce immunoglobulins. Different segments of DNA are mixed and matched randomly to create a new molecule. As illustrated in Figure 9, immunoglobulins consist of two different proteins—a heavy chain and a light chain. In the human heavy chain there are about forty different V (variable) segments, twenty-five different D (Diversity) segments, and six J (Joining) segments. The light chain also contains variable V and J segments. A completed immunoglobulin has a heavy chain with only one V, D, and J segment, and a light chain with only one V and D segment. It is the shuffling of these segments during development of the mature B lymphocyte that creates the diversity required (Figure 10). For example, there are about 8,000 heavy chain V, D,

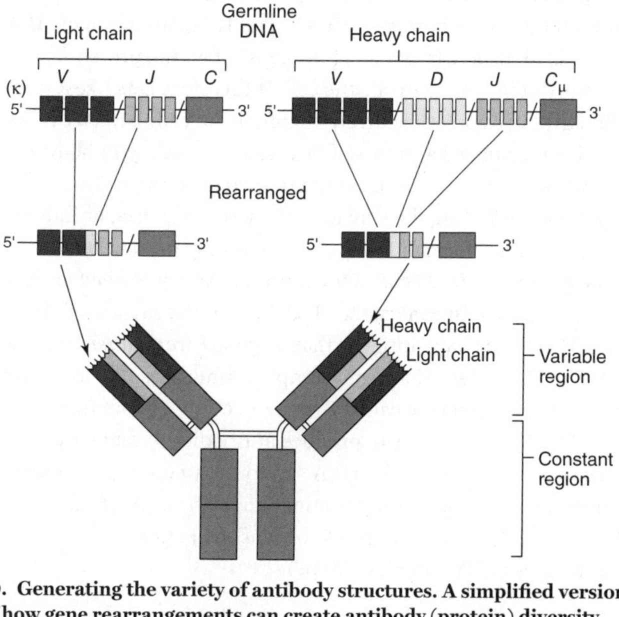

10. Generating the variety of antibody structures. A simplified version of how gene rearrangements can create antibody (protein) diversity. Many more secondary rearrangements are possible than can possibly be shown in this figure.

and J combinations and 300 light chain V and J combinations. Multiplying these numbers together, we get 2.4 million different immunoglobulin types. Even this is not enough to create the final diversity. To achieve this, the hypervariable regions are particularly susceptible to mutation during development. So each V, D, and J segment also differs subtly from the others, even before shuffling. This produces the additional variation needed to get almost a trillion different molecules. For 'his discovery of the genetic principle for generation of antibody diversity', Tonegawa won the Nobel Prize in 1987.

A separate class of immunoglobulin-like molecules also provide the key to cell-to-cell communication in the immune system. In humans, with the exception of the egg and sperm cells, all cells that possess a nucleus also have a protein on their surface called 'Human Leucocyte Antigen (HLA) Class I'. The function of HLA Class I is to display fragments (antigens) of all the proteins currently being made *inside* the cell. It therefore acts like a billboard displaying the current highlights of cellular activity. Any proteins recognized as non-self by cytotoxic T cell lymphocytes will result in the whole cell being targeted for destruction, hopefully preventing the spread of the virus, bacteria, or indeed cancer. Another form of HLA, Class II, is only present on the surface of specialized cells of the immune system termed antigen presenting cells. In contrast to HLA Class I, the surface of HLA Class II cells displays antigens that originate from *outside* of the cell. The HLA Class II antigen complex stimulates the production of a type of lymphocyte called 'T-helper cells', which in turn stimulate B lymphocytes to produce antibodies to that specific antigen. Mismatches in the HLA system between organ donors and recipients cause tissue rejection during transplantation. Hence the HLA system is also known as the major histocompatibility complex (MHC).

The modern view of the cells and molecules of the immune system is summarized in Figure 11. The innate (immediate) and adaptive

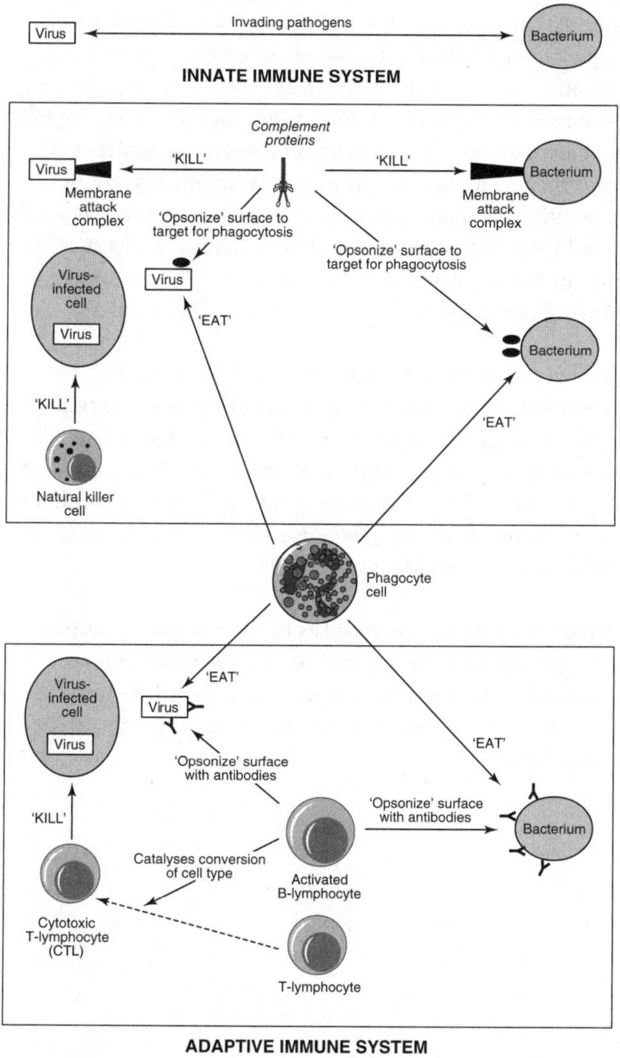

11. Comparing the innate and adaptive immune systems. A simplified diagram illustrating the innate (immediate) and adaptive (acquired) immune systems. Not shown are a range of accessory cells (e.g. T helper and B helper) and humoral components (including cytokines such as the interleukins and interferons).

(acquired) immune systems are linked by their shared use of phagocytic white blood cells. Both have cellular and humoral (molecular) components. Both target ('opsonize') invaders for destruction by the 'professional' phagocytes such as neutrophils and macrophages. The innate immune system opsonizes with complement components, whereas the acquired system uses antibodies. The innate system can also kill using direct molecular attack by forming a 'membrane attack complex' or direct cellular attack by the use of 'natural killer cells'. The adaptive system additionally uses cytotoxic T lymphocytes (CTL) to kill.

At first glance even such a very simplified illustration of the modern view of the cells and molecules of the immune system would be incomprehensible to both Ehrlich and Metchnikoff. However, it is likely they both would have seen the beauty in the complex interaction between the innate and acquired immunity, while perhaps still arguing about the relative importance of the cellular and humoral immune systems.

In Chapter 4 we return to blood as the body's transportation superhighway, focusing in particular on the most important molecule that it transports, oxygen. The story of how blood carries this gas from the lungs to the rest of the body is worth a chapter in its own right.

Chapter 4
Haemoglobin

What is haemoglobin?

Present at very high concentration inside erythrocytes, the protein haemoglobin absorbs light at the blue, green, and yellow end of the visible spectrum. What is left, to be reflected and viewed by the onlooker, is red light. Hence the erythrocyte's colour and more familiar name of the 'red blood cell'. Haemoglobin is more than just a pretty colour though. It plays the key role of binding oxygen in the lungs and carrying it around as the blood circulates, where it is offloaded to every cell in the body. The oxygen gas is then converted to water, a process that helps to deliver the chemical energy required for life.

Oxygen transport defines the primary biological function of blood. And red defines its primary cultural effect. No oxygen to cells means no energy, and death by stroke, trauma, or heart attack. No red colour means no 'red mist' to descend on an enraged football player, no one can be caught 'red-handed', and, of course, there would be no red stop signs. Therefore, the red oxygen carrying haemoglobin underpins both the biology and the culture of blood.

It was known from the early 19th century that blood contained more oxygen than could possibly be dissolved in water, and that most of it was bound to a red material. Chemists showed that the red pigment contained a protein bound to an organic porphyrin cofactor. This cofactor contained iron and was shown to be responsible for giving blood its red colour. It was called 'haem' (Figure 12). The colourless protein mass was called 'globin'. Combining these words, the great German chemist and physiologist, Felix Hoppe-Seyler, first coined the term 'haemoglobin' in 1864. The colour, iron content, and ability to form red crystals rapidly led to haemoglobin becoming the standard detection method for blood in forensic science. To this day, sprays that can detect the reactivity of haemoglobin remain a key method for determining the presence of blood at crime scenes.

Haemoglobin is of crucial biological importance; it is also easy to obtain safely in large quantities from donated blood. These properties have resulted in its becoming the most studied protein in human history.

Haemoglobin played a key role in the history of our understanding of all proteins, and indeed the science of biochemistry itself. In the

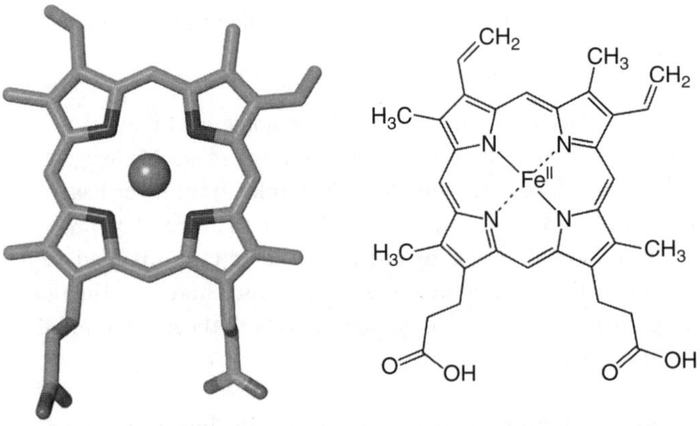

12. The structure of haem. Structural (left) and chemical (right) views of haem, showing the iron surrounded by its organic porphyrin cofactor.

mid-19th century chemists had sneered at this new discipline of studying the molecules of life—calling it 'Schmierchemie' or 'messy chemistry'. Yet the simple process of mixing blood with water, and then adding acid, changed all that. Beautiful red crystals were formed, similar in shape and structure to those formed by the simple well-defined molecules chemists were used to studying. By the early 20th century over 600 animal species had been shown to form these blood red crystals. Biochemists were no longer people who studied a mass of inhomogeneous ill-defined colloids; just like real chemists, they investigated real identifiable molecules that could form defined structures.

As an aside, scientists can get carried away by the ease of crystallization of haemoglobin. Although DNA can survive in ancient material, intact protein is less stable. Nevertheless haemoglobin is one of the few proteins present in large enough quantities to survive in archaeological material. Useful information has been obtained, for example, from fragments of haemoglobin recovered from the bones of soldiers buried in the Ancient Roman capital of Britain—Colchester.

Crystals such as those of common salt contain only two atoms (sodium and chlorine) forming a simple repeating cube. But a haemoglobin crystal contains over 10,000 atoms. Its three-dimensional structure is therefore far more complex. Unravelling this structure had to wait until 1936, when an Austrian émigré, Max Perutz, arrived in Cambridge, England. From this date until his death in 2002, Perutz worked on understanding the relationship of structure and function in haemoglobin.

The Second World War delayed the start of Perutz's research; classified as an enemy alien he was interned on the Isle of Wight. However, realizing they were wasting a valuable asset, the British authorities soon released him, enabling him to play a key role in Project Habakkuk. The project took its name from a verse in the Bible (Habakkuk 1:5)—'be utterly amazed, for I am going to do something in your days that you would not believe, even if you were told'. Project Habakkuk was indeed amazing; it attempted to build a floating airbase in the middle of the Atlantic Ocean using pykrete—a mixture of wood pulp and ice. The ultimate failure of this bizarre project was both scientific (although pykrete is much more resistant to melting than ice, it still needs an extensive cooling system) and political (Portugal allowed the Allies to use its airfields in the Azores, removing the need for a floating base).

Perutz returned after the war to work in the Cavendish laboratory in Cambridge. Here a technique called 'X-ray crystallography' was being used to determine the structure of complex molecules. Perutz successfully solved the three-dimensional structure of haemoglobin in 1960. Along with John Kendrew—who had solved the structure of the simpler muscle-oxygen carrying protein myoglobin in 1958—Perutz was awarded the Nobel Prize in Chemistry in 1962. This was the same year two other members of the same Cambridge laboratory, James Watson and Francis Crick, shared the Nobel Prize in Physiology and Medicine for their determination of the structure of the genetic material DNA. Biochemistry was officially no longer messy—indeed, over 30 per cent of the Nobel Prizes in Chemistry since that date have been awarded to biochemists, with many more awarded the Nobel Prize for Physiology or Medicine.

The 1962 Nobel Prizes were linked by more than the laboratory where the work was done. Like all proteins, the haemoglobin structure consists of a string of twenty different amino acids linked together in a sequence coded in strict order by the genetic material, DNA. Each gene codes for a different sequence of amino acids. Every protein therefore has a unique structure, which is linked to its unique function within the body. The linear sequence of amino acids is termed the 'primary structure'. These then interact to form local structures such as helices or sheets (secondary structure). In the case of globin proteins there are eight characteristic amino helices forming a characteristic fold (tertiary structure). Finally the haem cofactor is inserted. This completes the structure of myoglobin, the oxygen binding protein inside the muscle cell.

However, the situation with haemoglobin is more complex. Two separate, but very similar, genes code for haemoglobin. The resulting proteins produced, termed the 'alpha' and 'beta' subunits, bind together tightly forming a structure called a 'dimer'. Each dimer then binds to itself, forming a tetramer. The combination of the four protein subunits into a complex whole is termed the 'quaternary structure' of haemoglobin (Figure 13). A haemoglobin tetramer therefore contains four haem groups and can bind four molecules of oxygen.

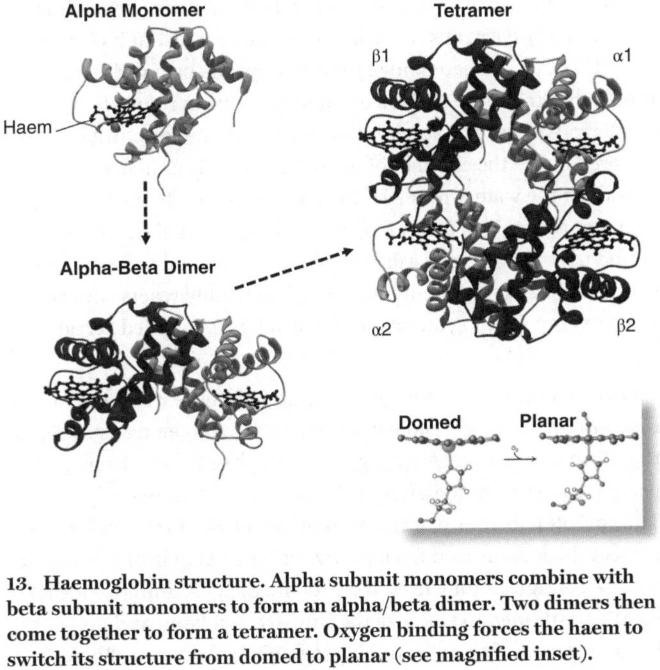

13. Haemoglobin structure. Alpha subunit monomers combine with beta subunit monomers to form an alpha/beta dimer. Two dimers then come together to form a tetramer. Oxygen binding forces the haem to switch its structure from domed to planar (see magnified inset).

Haemoglobin and oxygen

Oxygen gas consists of two atoms of oxygen bound together to form a symmetrical molecule. However, oxygen cannot be transported in the plasma alone. This is because water is very poor at dissolving oxygen. Haemoglobin's primary function is to increase this solubility; it does this by binding the oxygen gas on to the iron in its haem group. Every haem can bind one oxygen molecule, increasing the amount of oxygen able to dissolve in the blood. However, why is such a complex protein structure required to carry such a simple two-atom molecule like oxygen around the body in the first place? The key lies in the chemistry of the interaction of oxygen with the haem iron.

An iron atom can exist in a number of different forms depending on how many electrons it has in its atomic orbitals. In its ferrous (iron II) state iron can bind oxygen readily. The haemoglobin protein has therefore evolved to stabilize its haem iron cofactor in this ferrous state. The result is that over fifty times as much oxygen is stored inside the confines of the red blood cell compared to outside in the watery plasma. However, using iron to bind oxygen comes at a cost. Iron (II) can readily lose one of its electrons to the bound oxygen, a process called 'oxidation'. So the same form of iron that can bind oxygen avidly (ferrous) also readily reacts with that same oxygen forming an unreactive iron III state, called 'ferric'.

This oxidation is the same process that makes the iron in a car rust; simply using any old ferrous iron as an oxygen transporter is therefore impractical. A strong reductant, like ferrous iron, is primed to react immediately with a strong oxidant like oxygen. The complex structure of the protein haemoglobin is required to protect the ferrous iron from oxidizing. The haem iron is held in a precise configuration within the protein. Specific amino acids are ideally positioned to stabilize the iron–oxygen bond and prevent it from oxidizing. The haem in haemoglobin is therefore able to exist in two stable ferrous iron forms—the bright red coloured oxyhaemoglobin and the claret coloured deoxyhaemoglobin. Oxygen binding converts deoxyhaemoglobin to oxyhaemoglobin; the iron stays ferrous despite the presence of the nearby oxygen. Having evolved over many hundreds of millions of years, this stability is very difficult for chemists to mimic in the laboratory. This is one reason why, desirable as it might be in terms of cost and convenience, it is not currently possible to replace blood transfusions with a simple small chemical iron oxygen carrier.

The structure of the haemoglobin protein therefore stabilizes the iron–oxygen bond, allowing safe transportation of the reactive gas from the lungs to the tissue. Having four subunits means being able to carry four molecules of oxygen rather than one. However, the four subunits do more than enhance oxygen solubility. The quaternary structure allows for a delicate fine-tuning of oxygen transport to the specific requirements of the body at any specific time—a process called 'allostery', first discovered by a team of French and American scientists in Paris.

While Perutz was busy designing iceberg airstrips in the Second World War, elsewhere a French scientist, Jacques Monod, was fighting in the French Resistance, reaching the eventual rank of chief of staff of de Gaulle's French Forces of the Interior. Monod was a multi-talented scientist. After the War, his work on the control of gene activation won him a share of the 1965 Nobel Prize for Physiology and Medicine. But he was equally active in protein research. In the same year he won his Nobel, together with Jeffries Wyman and Jean-Pierre Changeux at the Pasteur Institute, Monod proposed his allosteric model of haemoglobin regulation (named MWC after the initials of its founders). This proposes that the quaternary structure of the haemoglobin tetramer can exist in two distinct structural forms: Relaxed (R) and Tense (T). They differ in that the R state binds oxygen more tightly than the T state. Effector molecules can bind to haemoglobin and stabilize one or other form of the protein. This will alter the ratio of R to T.

So if a molecule stabilizes the R state this will result in a larger proportion of the haemoglobin molecules in the R, rather than the T state; and vice versa, of course.

This structural switch might seem complex. But within the complexity lies a beautiful simplicity in linking protein structure to function and regulation (Figure 14). First of all in the lungs haemoglobin will be 100 per cent in the R state; all four subunits

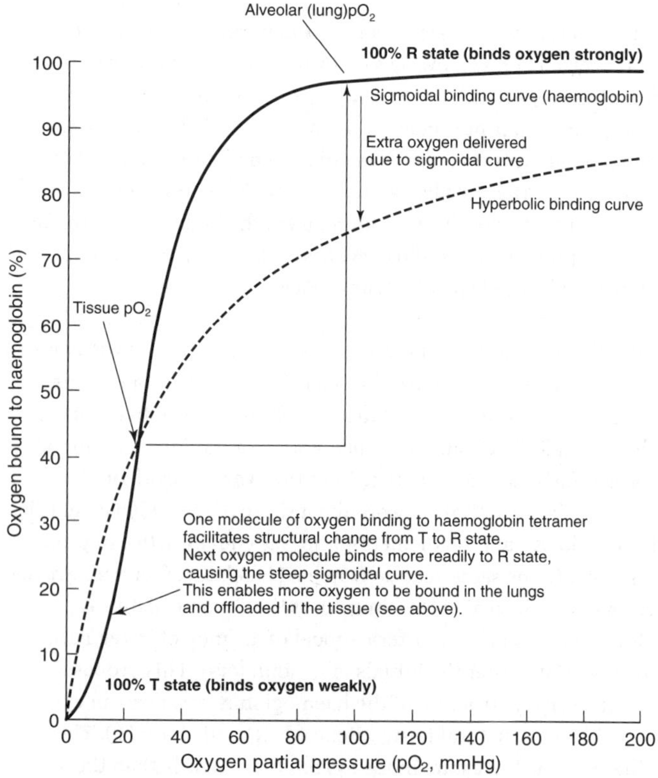

14. Oxygen binding by haemoglobin. A graph illustrating the fraction of oxygen binding to haemoglobin as oxygen tension varies.

will have oxygen tightly bound to them. As oxygen molecules are released to the tissue the balance shifts from the tight oxygen binding R state to the weak oxygen binding T state. This means that release of one oxygen molecule from a haemoglobin tetramer facilitates the release of the next oxygen as the protein is now more likely to be in the weak binding T state. This results in the characteristic sigmoidal or 's' shape of the oxygen binding curve. This ensures that the form of haemoglobin in the lungs (R state) is able to bind oxygen tightly and take it from the high partial pressure in the air. However, in the tissue the T state predominates; it binds oxygen more weakly, allowing the maximum amount of oxygen to be released to the regions of low oxygen pressure where it is most needed.

When Perutz looked at the three-dimensional structure it became clear how this process had evolved. The organic porphyrin is a planar ring structure. In the R state of haemoglobin, the iron atom at the centre of this ring sits slightly above the plane (illustrated in Figure 13). Once oxygen is bound to the iron it is energetically favourable for the atom to move down towards the plane. This movement in turn pulls amino acids near the iron towards the ring. In a kind of 'molecular domino' effect, a wide variety of other interactions are perturbed, including crucially those at the interface between the alpha and beta subunits. Thus an action at one of the four protein subunits can be converted into a concerted structural change that affects all of them. The R to T state change is best seen in a colour video, for example <http://biochem.web.utah.edu/iwasa/projects/hemoglobin.html>.

The haemoglobin structure enables the body to subtly and appropriately regulate its oxygen binding to suit environmental changes. As the R and T states have different structures they bind small molecules differently; as a consequence, allosteric effectors can elegantly control the oxygen affinity via preferentially binding, and hence stabilizing, the R or T states of the protein. For example, organs of the body that receive low levels of oxygen produce excess lactic acid. Elsewhere, where oxygen consumption is proceeding very quickly, a lot of carbon dioxide is produced. Both these conditions can co-exist in certain conditions such as intense exercise. In these circumstances the blood circulation needs to supply more oxygen to these tissues. In 1904 the Danish physiologist Christian Bohr discovered that under conditions of high carbon dioxide or increased acidity, haemoglobin decreases its affinity for oxygen, enabling those tissues to be preferentially targeted for enhanced oxygen delivery (Figure 15).

Named the Bohr effect, this process was probably responsible for saving the life of Christian's more famous son, the Nobel Prize winning physicist Niels Bohr. In 1943, when travelling from neutral Sweden to visit Winston Churchill in England, Bohr was instructed to put on his oxygen mask when the plane flew to high altitude over German occupied Norway. He did not

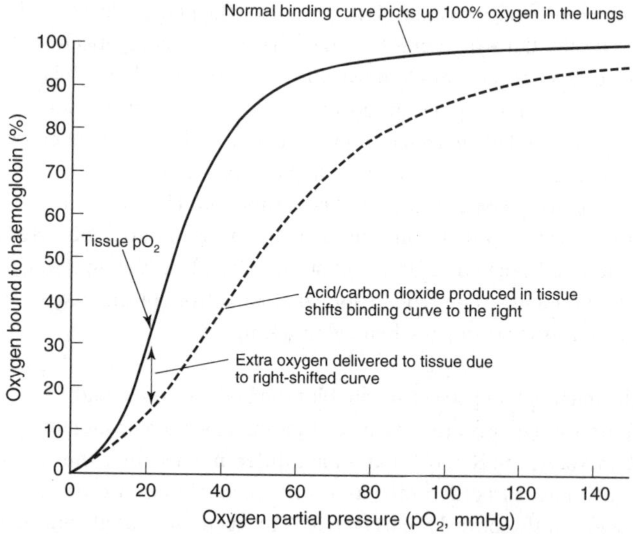

15. The Bohr effect. Acid and carbon dioxide facilitate oxygen offloading to tissue.

hear this instruction (the story is that Bohr could not wear a helmet with a built-in intercom system as his head was too big). Consequently, Niels passed out due to lack of oxygen. This triggered a number of physiological defence responses to protect his brain, one of which would have been the haemoglobin Bohr effect named after his father (Christian). Bohr the younger recovered when the plane descended over the North Sea, later playing a role in the Manhattan project that built the first atom bombs.

It took over fifty years for biochemists to come up with a molecular explanation for the Bohr effect. It was shown that the binding of protons (acid) or bicarbonate (produced from carbon dioxide) stabilized the low affinity T state of the haemoglobin molecule. Therefore the protein has evolved such that in those tissues where oxygen is most needed, it is converted into the very form that offloads oxygen most readily. This was one of the earliest examples in which a physiological effect was explained by a biochemical description at the level of the individual atoms in the protein concerned.

The situation with another effector, bisphosphoglycerate (BPG), is more complex. BPG also favours the T state, so decreasing oxygen binding. In humans, BPG levels are used to fine-tune the haemoglobin oxygen affinity. When you climb to high altitudes the decreased oxygen partial pressure in the air triggers production of the hormone erythropoetin from the kidney; this in turn triggers the production of more red blood cells. But this process can take days or weeks to offset the oxygen deficit. The more immediate response to altitude is to increase the BPG levels in the blood. This increases the concentration of the haemoglobin T state. Although this has the desired effect of offloading more oxygen to the tissues that need it, there is a compromise. Slightly less oxygen will be able to be picked up in the lungs. If you climb too high, not even the wonders of biochemistry can overcome the decreased oxygen pressure in the air.

So far we have described examples of when the body requires a lower affinity haemoglobin. However, sometimes the reverse is the case and more high affinity R state haemoglobin is required. This is the case in the foetus, where the only supply of oxygen is from the maternal blood supply. In order to capture the oxygen from its mother the foetus has a special form of haemoglobin in which the beta subunit is replaced by a subtly different gamma subunit. This is still able to bind to the alpha subunit, but the resultant haemoglobin protein is less responsive to BPG. The R state is therefore favoured and oxygen can be 'stolen' from the mother. Interestingly evolution has solved this conundrum in different ways. Whereas in the human a new form of haemoglobin is synthesized that cannot bind BPG, in the cow the foetus has exactly the same haemoglobin as its mother, but achieves the higher affinity by having much lower BPG levels in the foetal circulation.

The evolution of haemoglobin

Throughout evolution this globin plus iron combination has proved adaptable to a wide variety of habitats and environments. For example, Nile crocodiles have a form of haemoglobin with an enhanced carbon dioxide Bohr effect. This enables them to hold their breath for over an hour as they drown their prey; in the 1980s Kiyoshi Nagai in Cambridge patented a human haemoglobin as a potential blood substitute that was re-engineered to resemble that of the crocodile, appropriately called 'Haemoglobin Scuba' (though unfortunately this was never made into an effective product). Even more surprising than the crocodile is the use that fish make of haemoglobin. The adult trout for example contains no fewer than four haemoglobins to adapt to different physiological conditions. The most intriguing use is linked to the function of the swim bladder. As noted by Darwin in *The Origin of Species*, this organ, present in all ray-finned fish, is homologous to the mammalian lung. It is a gas-filled chamber surrounded by blood vessels. These vessels, called the 'rete mirabile', or 'wonderful net', have the ability to pump acid into their blood supply under the control of the fish nervous system. One of the four trout haemoglobin proteins has an extreme Bohr effect with a very strong dependence of oxygen binding on blood acidity. Under acidic conditions, this haemoglobin can offload its oxygen into the swim bladder even at very high pressures. By controlling the amount of acid in the rete mirabile, the fish can consequently control the oxygen pressure in its swim bladder and hence its buoyancy. The allosteric effect of haemoglobin is therefore what enables fish with swim bladders to stay at a defined depth without the need to expend the energy of swimming.

Moving from the depths of the ocean to the highest peaks we find the bar-headed goose. This bird lives and hatches its young in Tibet, migrating over the peak of Mount Everest. Its haemoglobin has evolved to bind oxygen tightly at very low pressures; hence it can exercise at oxygen pressures less than a third of those available at sea level. It is humbling to compare this bird soaring freely above with the efforts expended by the humans struggling on the slopes below. In the words of Edward Norton, the first climber to reach 28,000 feet on Mount Everest in 1924, 'My ambition was to do twenty paces uphill without a pause to rest and pant, elbow on bent knee. Yet I never remember achieving it—thirteen was nearer the mark.' The lack of the correct haemoglobin meant that humans would have to wait for thirty more years before going higher to the summit of the mountain, assisted by the development of suitable portable oxygen supplies.

Evolution does not always require haemoglobin to be packaged inside a red blood cell. The main reason this has arisen in mammals is that, left free in the plasma, the protein would be excreted by the kidney and rapidly leave the circulation. However, many annelid worms (including the common earthworm) have no red blood cells and are perfectly happy allowing their haemoglobin to fend for itself in the circulation. This is made possible as they have evolved giant haemoglobin proteins called 'erythrocruorins'. These comprise as many as 144 separate globin protein subunits, stuck together with thirty-six linker subunits of a different protein. Such a megaprotein, well over a million atoms large, has no chance of leaking out of the circulation. Intriguingly, this ability to function happily outside a cell has led one adventurous French company, Hemarina, to patent the use of worm blood as an artificial red blood cell substitute in humans.

Large warm-blooded animals need to control their body temperature carefully. Blood plays a key part in this process. In humans, skin temperature is 4°C colder than the body's core temperature. Therefore as the body's metabolism creates heat, this dissipates as the blood flows through the skin. Varying the rate of skin blood flow (high when hot, low when cold) is a major part of the body's thermoregulatory system. However, at the 37°C temperature of the mother's womb, with no access to the outside world, the human foetus risks overheating as the heat generated by its metabolism has no mechanism of dissipation.

Enter haemoglobin. Haemoglobin is a very abundant protein in the body. Binding, delivering, and offloading oxygen consequently comprises a major part of the body's metabolism. Even small amounts of heat associated with oxygen binding and release can therefore contribute significantly to the total heat production of the body. The human foetus makes use of this to cool off by altering the heat associated with its binding of oxygen. Foetal haemoglobin has a lower heat associated with oxygen binding than adult haemoglobin; more heat is absorbed on dissociation of oxygen from maternal haemoglobin than is released when oxygen binds to foetal haemoglobin. Therefore the process of transferring oxygen from the mother to the foetus acts as a mechanism of cooling the foetus. In effect maternal haemoglobin brings both energy and air conditioning to the foetus. A similar process happens in animals that need to reduce heat due to an overactive metabolism. For example the heat released during the oxygen binding and release from the haemoglobin of migratory birds (such as water hens) is much larger than that of non-migratory species such as pigeons. The former can consequently fly for long distances without overheating.

The male penguin has the opposite problem, having to sit on the egg for months at a time. Why don't its feet freeze in winter? One part of the answer again relates to haemoglobin, as Antarctic penguins lose less heat than other animals when their haemoglobin is deoxygenated in the cold peripheral tissues. Some Antarctic fish actually have a positive heat of oxygenation. This process is taken to an extreme in the humble tuna fish. This fish has arranged heat changes associated with haemoglobin oxygen binding such that it can maintain its body temperature up to 17°C warmer than its environment, thus proving that not all fish are cold blooded.

In 2010, in a study almost worthy of the movie *Jurassic Park*, the haemoglobin gene was cloned from the well-preserved body of a woolly mammoth. The full protein was then 'resurrected' by scientists at the Australian Centre for Ancient DNA in Adelaide, collaborating with colleagues more used to the frozen North working out of Winnipeg in Manitoba. Compared to the Asian elephant of today, woolly mammoth haemoglobin was indeed shown to have genetic modifications that enabled oxygen delivery at a much lower temperature than would otherwise be possible.

Haemoglobin's relatives

Haemoglobin is not the only oxygen transport used in blood. Haemerythrin is a protein found inside some marine invertebrates, such as brachiopods, priapulids (penis worms), and sipunculans (peanut worms). Despite its name the protein has no attached haem group to bind the iron. Instead the iron is bound directly to the protein's amino acids. However, haemerythrin performs the same function—reversibly binding oxygen and transporting it around the body—although the absence of a haem cofactor means the blood cells are pink, rather than red. A different metal, copper, is used to bind oxygen in the haemocyanin protein found in some arthropods and molluscs, including some snails, spiders, scorpions, and centipedes. The protein is not found inside cells, instead being found suspended in the haemolymph, the invertebrate equivalent of blood. When oxygen binds to haemocyanin it turns blue; this is the reason why many invertebrates such as horseshoe crabs, lobsters, and octopi can be thought of as having 'blue blood'. The English phrase 'blue blooded' refers to the nobility, but this is not due to a rare haemoglobin-copper mutation in high-born families. Instead it is a literal translation of the Spanish 'sangre azul'. This was a term attributed to the oldest and proudest families of Castile, who claimed to have no dark Moorish blood in their veins. Of course, unlike lobsters, the blood flowing within the veins of the nobility is in fact the same dark red as that of you or me. The colour of the veins we see with our eyes is a complex optical integration of the colour of the blood itself and the skin it is reflected through. The same blood will therefore look darker when reflected through dark skin than it does through that of a 'noble' Castilian.

Given the success of the haem iron and globin combination in haemoglobin, it is no surprise that organisms have used this basic biochemical architecture for a variety of purposes throughout evolution, not just oxygen transport in blood. One example is the protein myoglobin. This protein resides inside animal cells; in the human it is found in the heart and skeletal muscle. It gives red meat its red colour, turning to brown as the haem iron is oxidized during the cooking process. Myoglobin has multiple functions. Its primary role is as an aid to oxygen diffusion. Whereas haemoglobin transports oxygen from the lung to the cell, myoglobin transports it once it is inside the cell. As oxygen is so poorly soluble in water, having a chain of molecules inside the cell that can bind and release oxygen rapidly significantly decreases the time it takes the gas to get from the blood capillary to the part of the cell—the mitochondria—where it is needed. To visualize how this could work, imagine a line of people putting out a fire by making a human chain to pass the buckets from water pump to fire. This is much faster than one person running from the pump to the fire and back again.

Myoglobin can also act as an emergency oxygen backup store. In humans this is trivial and of questionable importance. Not so in diving mammals such as whales and dolphins that have as much as thirty times the myoglobin content of the terrestrial equivalent; indeed those mammals that dive for the longest duration have the most myoglobin. This natural abundance is the reason that the myoglobin crystallized by Kendrew for his structural determinations in the 1950s came from the sperm whale. The human protein was only crystallized much later in the 1990s when the gene was cloned and the protein made by genetic modification techniques in *E. coli* bacteria.

The third known function of myoglobin is to protect the muscle cells from damage by nitric oxide gas. This molecule plays an important role as a naturally synthesized signalling molecule. However, in some pathologies too much nitric oxide is produced which can be highly reactive and dangerous to cells. The form of myoglobin with oxygen bound to it reacts rapidly with nitric oxide, converting it into a relatively harmless product, nitrate, and protecting the cell. The same chemistry is utilized by organisms when under attack by nitric oxide gas released by white blood cells. For example, the *E. coli* bacterium, in response to this biological gas attack, produces large amounts of a small haemoglobin-like protein (called 'Hmp') that converts the dangerous nitric oxide to nitrate.

The human genome project has enabled the classification of all the globin type proteins in the human body. In addition to myoglobin and haemoglobin, two others have been characterized, called 'cytoglobin' and 'neuroglobin'. As befits their name cytoglobin is found in all cells, whereas neuroglobin is generally restricted to nervous tissues. With the exception of the retina (where there is a large concentration of neuroglobin), these two proteins are present at too low an abundance to be important for oxygen transport. In fact their precise role in the body is still unclear. Neuroglobin seems to play a role in defence against brain damage (e.g. stroke), possibly utilizing some of the nitric oxide chemistry described earlier. Cytoglobin is more mysterious; one of the current suggestions is that it responds to cellular stress caused by reactive oxygen free radicals and triggers antioxidant defence mechanisms.

Haemoglobin and disease

As haemoglobin, and the related globin proteins, have evolved to perform a range of vital, complex functions in the body, changes in their structure can therefore have severe medical consequences. Most famous is the case of sickle cell disease. Louis Pasteur's work in the late 19th century demonstrated the germ theory of disease; microorganisms in the environment could cause disease. However, not all disease could be linked to microbes. Then in 1949 Linus Pauling showed that sickle cell disease was caused by an inherited alteration in a single protein—haemoglobin. This ushered in the age of molecular medicine and biochemists, and molecular geneticists rapidly became as important as microbiologists in clinical medicine.

The defect itself underlying sickle cell disease is the result of a single change in the DNA code of the beta haemoglobin subunit (called 'HbS'). This replaces an amino acid with a negative charge (glutamic acid) with one that is neutral (valine). This apparently very small change can have catastrophic consequences. The T state of haemoglobin favoured at low oxygen concentrations has a long patch of uncharged amino acids. The valine in sickle cell haemoglobin can 'stick' to this patch. This results in the aggregation of the haemoglobin protein. In and of itself this is not too problematic. However, there is so much haemoglobin in the red blood cell that a structural change in this protein can affect the structure of the entire red blood cell. Gone is the beautiful, flexible biconcave disk able to squeeze through the smallest capillary, replaced by the inflexible sickle shaped cell that gives the disease its name. Too many of these trigger a sickle cell crisis, occluding blood vessels and dramatically restricting blood flow.

The prevalence of sickle cell disease is coincident with parts of the world where malaria is present (Figure 16). This is one of the best examples of an apparently deleterious mutation that is favoured by natural selection. For the reasons discussed, having two copies of the sickle cell gene (from mother and father) has a poor prognosis. However, unless you are planning to be a mountaineer, having one copy is much less problematic—at least for the human being. Not so for the malarial parasite, which cannot readily

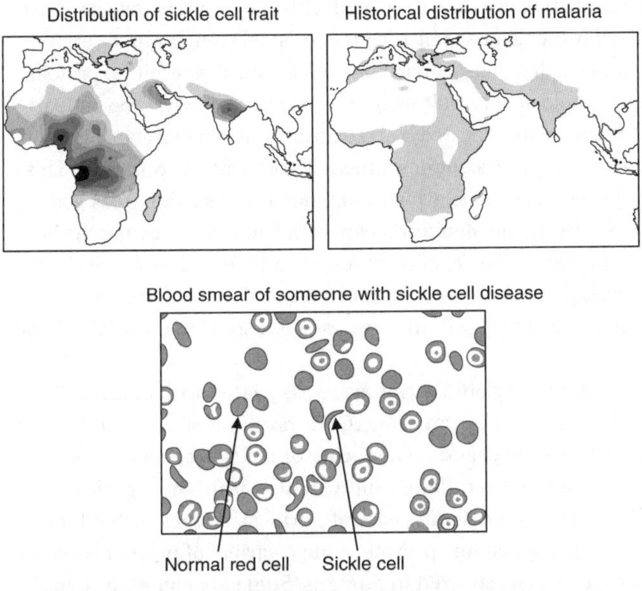

16. Coincidence of sickle cell disease and malaria. Coincidence of historical geographical distribution of malaria with that of the sickle cell gene (top); blood smear from patient with sickle cell disease (bottom).

parasitize cells containing HbS. The result is that, when faced with the threat of malarial parasites on a daily basis, having the 'good' gene from both parents is as bad as having 'bad' genes from both of them. The optimum balance is to have one of each, with the result that natural selection acts to preserve the HbS gene in the population. This balance can lead to apparently strange situations. For example in parts of Saudi Arabia the population maintains the foetal form of its haemoglobin well into adult life. This is because, as mentioned previously, in foetal haemoglobin the role of the beta subunit is replaced by a gamma subunit. Foetal haemoglobin therefore lacks the HbS mutation and cannot sickle; consequently partial resistance to malaria can be maintained without irreversible red cell damage.

Other pathologies are associated with haemoglobin defects, most notably the thalassaemias, caused by single mutations, or even complete deletions, of haemoglobin genes. The resultant proteins do not fold at all, resulting in severe anaemia, unless the patient is treated with repeated blood transfusions. Thalassaemia is particularly prevalent in southern Mediterranean countries. This is reflected in its name, which combines Thalassa, the Greek god personifying the Mediterranean, with haem representing the blood red pigment. The benefits are less clear than with sickle cell haemoglobin, but recent studies suggest that the defect leads to smaller red blood cells that are less susceptible to malarial infection.

Not all haemoglobin variants are associated with disease. The end of the 20th century saw the unravelling of the genetic code via large-scale genetic sequencing of DNA from a variety of species and from different individuals within that species. However, haemoglobin's ease of purification meant that long before these genome projects a huge variety of protein variants had been characterized in humans. Some are common, some rare, some benign and some damaging (the latter make up the haemoglobinopathies). They are generally named after the town where they were first discovered, rather than the person who provided the blood. From Hb Essex to Hb Karachi to Hb Swan River, over 1,180 different variants are known. They are mostly one-off mutations and hence know no geographic boundaries. Identities are sometimes contested. For example Hb Cambridge named after an English family is identical to Hb Rambam found in a member of a Bedouin tribe in Israel. Rambam is named after the hospital where it was discovered, which in turn was named after a famous Jewish scholar. The same mutation has since been discovered in Argentina and Germany.

Sickle cell disease, the thalassaemias, and the haemoglobinopathies are caused by changes in the globin part of the protein. However, the same Hope-Seyler who discovered haemoglobin explained the biochemistry underpinning diseases associated with a purple pigment (porphyria) appearing in faeces and urine. Here there is a defect in the manufacture of the haem that is added to the globin; this is now known to be caused by mutations in the enzymes required by the body to manufacture the organic porphyrin. The problem in these diseases is not, however, that there is insufficient haem to combine with the globin protein to form haemoglobin. Just about enough seems to be made. However, it is made so slowly that some of the intermediates in haem biosynthesis build up to toxic levels. One of the symptoms of acute porphyria is mental illness. It has been suggested, on admittedly rather scanty evidence, that the English king, George III, suffered from this disease—hence the obsessive monitoring of the colour of royal stools in the movie *The Madness of King George*.

Haemoglobin as a diagnostic tool

Although restricted to one cell type, haemoglobin is still one of the most common proteins in the body. Its abundance and unusual physical properties combine to make it an ideal tool for scientists to use to probe human biology and medicine. For example, when oxygen binds, the claret coloured deoxyhaemoglobin is converted to bright red oxyhaemoglobin. This colour change can be used to

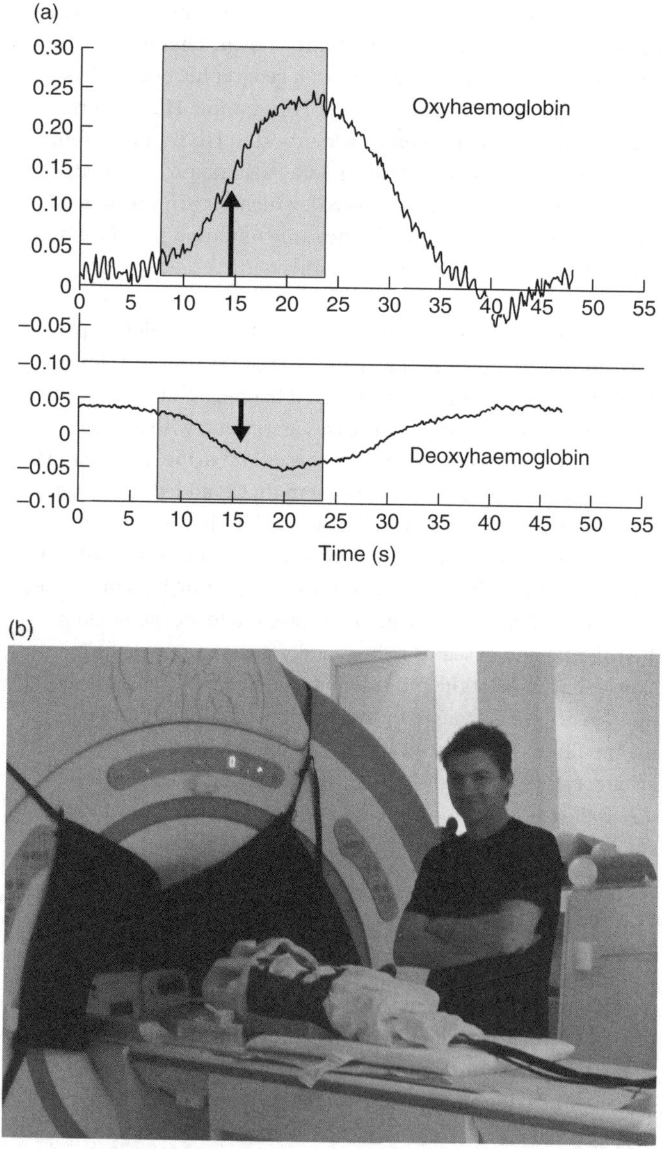
(a)
0.30
0.25
0.20
0.15
0.10
0.05
0
−0.05
−0.10
Oxyhaemoglobin
0.05
0
−0.05
−0.10
Deoxyhaemoglobin
0 5 10 15 20 25 30 35 40 45 50 55
Time (s)
(b)

(c)

17. Using blood to study brain function. (a) Stimulation of the brain by a visual stimulus (shaded region of graph) causes an increase in oxyhaemoglobin and a decrease in deoxyhaemoglobin concentration in the brain; measured in micromolar units. Photos illustrate the use of (b) magnetic (fMRI) and (c) optical (fNIRS) properties of haemoglobin to study brain function in infants.

measure the oxygen saturation of arterial blood (i.e. what proportion of the haemoglobin has oxygen bound). As red light passes readily through tissues this can be done non-invasively by attaching a device called a 'pulse oximeter' on a human finger. The colour change linked to the arterial pulse indicates how much oxygen has been bound to deoxyhaemoglobin as it passes through the lungs. This is crucial information for patients who may be suffering an asthma attack or who are being artificially ventilated during a surgical operation or on intensive care. Near Infrared (NIR) light of longer wavelengths penetrates even deeper into tissue and can report on the oxygenation in the muscles of athletes during exercise or in the brain of patients during surgery.

Historically the knowledge of which part of the brain was actively responding to stimuli required direct electrical measurements on exposed animal brains or conscious patients during brain surgery. However, this has changed dramatically in the past twenty years, leading to a revolution in neuroscience. Haemoglobin is not just coloured. In its deoxygenated form it is paramagnetic. The amount of deoxyhaemoglobin in the blood therefore affects the magnetic properties of the nearby water molecules. This can be picked up by functional Magnetic Resonance Imaging (fMRI). Changes in brain blood flow decrease the amount of deoxyhaemoglobin in the region of the brain that is being activated (Figure 17). Consequently fMRI maps of brain activity can indicate in real time how the brain responds to which stimulus (e.g. light, sound, emotion, cognition). Functional connections between different brain regions can also be mapped. The equivalent optical tool (fNIRS) is now enabling lower resolution functional maps to be measured outside the confines of the MRI magnet, particularly useful in studies on brain development in infants.

In the preceding chapters, we have learnt that blood combines the ultimate oxygen transportation system with the ability to pack a punch to attack invaders. But what of the engine that drives blood around the body and what happens when the engine fails?

Chapter 5
Blood pressure and blood flow

Measuring blood pressure

The heart is the organ that pumps blood around the body. If the heart stops functioning, blood does not flow. The driving force for this flow is the pressure difference between the arterial blood leaving the heart and the returning venous blood. The decreasing pressure in the venous side explains the need for unidirectional valves within veins to prevent the blood flowing in the wrong direction. Without them the return of the blood through the veins to the heart would be too slow, especially when standing up, when the venous pressure struggles to overcome gravity.

The existence of venous valves was one of the key pieces of evidence William Harvey used to confirm the existence of the blood circulation system (see Chapter 1). However, although Harvey knew about blood flow, he would not have formally phrased the force driving it as a 'pressure', because the relationship between pressure and flow in fluids was not formulated quantitatively until a hundred years after Harvey published *De Motu Cordis*. It took the Swiss mathematician and physicist Daniel Bernoulli in his book *Hydrodynamica* to demonstrate formally in 1738 that if fluid is flowing from a region of high pressure to a region of lower pressure, the increased pressure behind gives a net force on the liquid, accelerating its flow. Bernoulli was one member of an amazing mathematical family; over three generations eight members of this family distinguished themselves in applied mathematics and physics. Named after one or other of this family are: Bernoulli distribution; Bernoulli number; Bernoulli polynomials; Bernoulli process; Bernoulli trial; Bernoulli principle; and even the Bernoulli Society for Mathematical Statistics.

Daniel Bernoulli measured pressure by puncturing the wall of a vessel with an open-ended straw; the higher the fluid rose up the straw against the force of atmospheric pressure, the higher the pressure in the vessel. Despite being trained in medicine, there is no evidence that Bernoulli ever used arteries as 'vessels' in his studies. However, at about the same time, an English clergyman and scientist, Stephen Hales, became interested in fluid movement in plants and animals. Hales was already well known in English scientific circles for publishing one of the first books on plant physiology—*Vegetable Statiks*. This included measurements of the 'force of the sap' or root pressure. It was but a short step from here to the sequel *Haemastatiks*. Published in 1733 this contained the first ever measurement of blood pressure.

It was hardly non-invasive (Figure 18), consisting of tying a horse down on its back and opening an artery in its thigh. Into this was inserted a sixth of an inch diameter brass pipe. The pipe was attached to a nine foot glass tube. Blood flowed up the tube to a height of 8 feet and 3 inches, rising and falling 2 or 3 inches with each pulse. Hales was not completely comfortable with his move from plant to animal physiology; he was slow in following up his discovery due to the 'disagreeableness of Anatomical dissections'. However, his place as the discoverer of blood pressure was assured.

The method Hales devised of directly sampling in an artery is still the most effective and robust method for measuring blood pressure over 300 years later. Nowadays it involves inserting a catheter into an artery (an 'arterial line') and linking this to an electronic pressure transducer. This has the advantage that it

18. Artist's impression of the first blood pressure measurement.

allows for continuous real time measurements. However, the disadvantage is that it is invasive and therefore used only in hospital situations, for example during surgery.

Everyone will be familiar with the non-invasive measurement that makes use of a blood pressure cuff inflated on the arm. This method, based on measuring the pressure required to stop the pulsation of an artery, was first suggested in 1855 by the German physician Karl von Vierordt. His device, involving weights and levers to apply the counter pressure, was cumbersome, but by the end of the century more practical devices had been developed. There was resistance to their use, however, with the august *British Medical Journal* declaring that 'by using the sphygmomanometer [blood pressure monitor] we pauperize our senses and weaken clinical acuity'. Interestingly, even today the clinical value of an overreliance on blood pressure monitoring in acute hospital care is questioned—although usually from the viewpoint that a more advanced piece of monitoring equipment should be used instead.

The arterial pulsation method does not require the insertion of a needle into an artery. In its modern incarnation, a cuff is first placed on the arm and then inflated to above arterial pressure. This (temporarily) completely stops blood flow to the region of arm below the cuff. This process is completely safe as, unlike the brain, muscle and skin are organs that can survive without oxygen for many minutes. The air is slowly let out from the cuff and the applied pressure drops. At the same time a stethoscope is used to listen to the noise that is made by turbulence when the blood starts to flow again through the compressed vessel (called 'Korotkoff sounds'). This happens when the externally applied pressure and the internal blood pressure are equal. This pressure is called the 'systolic pressure'. However, the heart is not a continuous pump; it pumps with a beat. At the peak of the beat the pressure is maximum; when the heart is not beating it is at a minimum. We don't have a single blood pressure—it varies continuously. Therefore the sound of the blood flowing through the stethoscope will also fluctuate; the point when the cuff pressure is so low that the blood flows continuously, and turbulence is no longer heard, marks the lowest pressure in the system—that between heart beats.

The time when the heart beats is called a 'systole'. The time when the heart is refilling with blood is called diastole. Therefore, the peak pressure measured is called 'systolic pressure' and the lowest pressure diastolic. Blood pressure is thus usually recorded as two numbers (systolic over diastolic). Clinicians and nurses may calculate a mean arterial pressure (MAP). This is the mean pressure over the cardiac (heart beat) cycle. With a normal heart rate, systole is approximately half the duration of diastole so the mean pressure is a third of the difference between diastole and systole. If blood pressure becomes too low, flow is compromised and organs can become damaged.

In Figure 19, a real time blood pressure tracing is shown along with the sounds heard through the stethoscope. The first sound indicates systolic pressure. As more air is released from the cuff, blood is able to flow freely through the brachial artery and all sounds disappear. The point at which the last sound is heard is

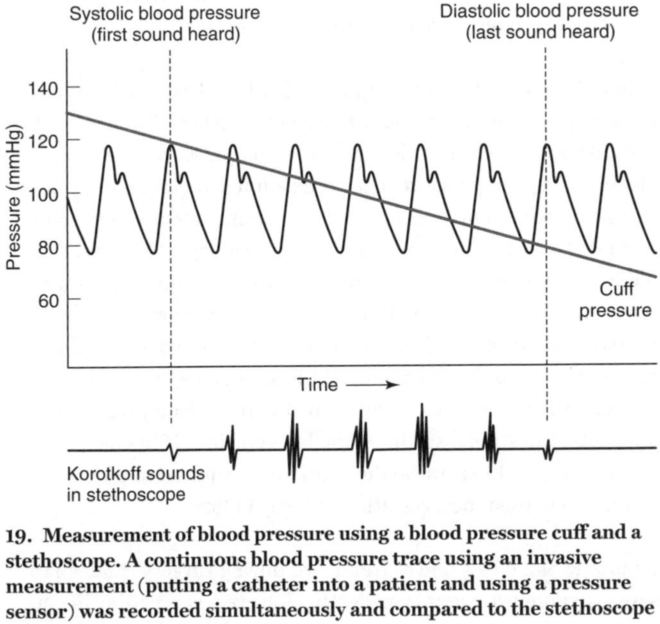

19. Measurement of blood pressure using a blood pressure cuff and a stethoscope. A continuous blood pressure trace using an invasive measurement (putting a catheter into a patient and using a pressure sensor) was recorded simultaneously and compared to the stethoscope recordings.

recorded as the patient's diastolic pressure. Current monitors vary the applied cuff pressure automatically. Between the systolic and diastolic pressures, oscillations can be detected using an electronic pressure sensor; mathematical algorithms are then used to calculate the patient's blood pressure values. The need for human intervention in the process is therefore completely removed. One wonders what the elders of the *British Medical Journal* would have thought about this.

Blood pressure and health

The revolution in technology makes it relatively easy to obtain an accurate reading. Blood pressure measurements can now even be done remotely in a patient's home. However, the doctor is not sidelined. The key question is what to do with that number once you have it? Advances in medical technology just move the human interface to a later stage in the diagnostic process.

What about blood pressure in everyday life? Unusually for a physiological measurement, many people—especially over a certain age—have some idea of their blood pressure. The normal 'healthy' range of pressure in a young adult is defined as a systolic pressure between 90 and 120 and a diastolic pressure between 60 and 80. These normal ranges rise slowly with age. Given that blood pressure drives blood flow and tissues absolutely require blood for survival, one might even expect that a higher blood pressure (hypertension) would be better than the opposite (low blood pressure or hypotension). While often true, the high resistance in the arterial circulation at higher blood pressures does place additional strain on the left ventricle. If the heart is weak, it may fail to achieve the extra force required to pump against this resistance, resulting in heart failure.

Dramatic blood loss due to trauma or during surgery can lead to severe hypotension and even death. However, in everyday life, a low blood pressure is rarely of concern. Indeed, it can be a sign of fitness as elite athletes have a much lower resting blood pressure than the rest of the population. This appears counter-intuitive as high performance sport requires elevated heart rates and blood pressure to support optimum blood flow and oxygen delivery to exercising tissues. However, the effect of exercise training is to thicken the muscles in the walls of the heart and enlarge the chambers. This enables more blood to be pumped per beat during intense exercise. The consequence of this extra efficiency is that when an athlete is resting—and therefore needs no more oxygen than a more sedentary person—the heart rate and blood pressure are lower than average.

Most people's experience of hypotension will be reflected by dizzy spells and lack of balance, especially when moving quickly to an upright position. This is because more blood pools in the legs when you stand up, meaning there is less blood for the heart to pump. The immediate effect should be for the heart to beat faster to restore the pressure. If there is a delay, the decrease in pressure can decrease the blood flow to the brain and cause dizziness; in extreme cases this can lead to fainting. This has the advantage of being self-correcting as the blood that has pooled in the legs is once again distributed around the body.

In marked contrast to hypotension, approximately a third of the population in the developed world have hypertension—as defined by a systolic pressure over 140 or a diastolic above 90 (140/90). Chronic (lifelong) hypertension has serious long-term adverse health consequences. Over $50 billion is spent worldwide on drugs designed to decrease pressures above 140/90 back to a 'normal' healthy range. Concerns over high blood pressure are not restricted to the present day. Historical records talk of a 'hard pulse disease'. Feeling the pulse was an established practice of doctors throughout the ages, well before the mechanism of pulsing was appreciated. The great champion in Britain, Sir John Floyer, published two influential essays in 1707 and 1710 (*The Physician's Pulse Watch*, Volumes I and II). The first focused on measuring the pulse and how it could be improved using a special watch he designed that ran for precisely 60 seconds. The second volume covered the use of pulse measurement, describing different pathologies and how they could be diagnosed. Floyer asserted that there was far more to a pulse than just its speed. A pulse could be small, unequal, intermittent, languid, soft, undulous, or broad; pathologies such as flatulence, scurvy, pleurisy, jaundice, and epilepsy were associated with different pulse descriptions. Traditional Chinese medicine goes even further, listing as many as twenty-eight different types of pulse.

Though modern Western medicine would baulk at the number of subcategories, it is indeed true that a skilled practitioner can gain useful information by careful palpation of the pulse. In particular the so-called 'hard' pulse is felt when the pressure is high. In a hard pulse the artery feels firm when it pulses, almost like a taut string. Therefore it is possible to make a crude diagnosis of hypertension by merely feeling the pulse. Historical descriptions of 'hard pulse disease' go back over 4,000 years, to semi-mythical figures such as the Chinese Yellow Emperor. The Emperor, along with later doctors such as Galen and Floyer, apparently advocated bloodletting or treatment with leeches as a cure for this condition. For once, the bleeders might actually have been on to something; the hard pulse caused by high blood pressure is one of the few conditions that can be normalized by removing blood. Fewer blood cells will result in a lower pressure. Still, the amount of blood that would need to be removed to have a positive long-term effect on blood pressure would be significant, and the bloodletting would do nothing to affect the long-term problems, which would undoubtedly return.

Due to the difficulties in routine measurements, medicine was naturally slow to shift from measurements of the blood pulse to measurements of blood pressure. However, by the early 20th century hypertension became a quantified and recognized pathology. The state of the field was well summarized by Dr John Hay in a British

Medical Association lecture given in 1931. This is a prescient and well-argued lecture. Much of what Hay states has stood the test of time, though perhaps not his division of patients into three archetypes: spare sallow, highly strung individuals with a tendency to constipation and a coated tongue; florid stoutish muscular persons with a vigorous mentality, an excellent appetite, good digestion, and a clean tongue; and finally the menopausal group, characterized by an obesity hard to dispel.

Treating high blood pressure

We now know that early onset hypertension (before age 50) is associated with a doubling of the risk of death from heart disease. However, Hay cautioned against too rigid an intervention, famously stating 'There is some truth in the saying that the greatest danger to a man with a high blood pressure lies in its discovery, because then "some fool is certain to try and reduce it"'. He noted the correlation with an overindulgent diet, obesity, and lack of exercise in his patients; hypertension was, in many cases, the penalty of success for the successful man who rode rather than walked and was overworked and stressed. Many of the work–life balance and dietary recommendations of the time are identical to what is deemed current best practice: reducing workplace stress; exercise; a decrease in alcohol and tobacco intake; a decrease in fatty foods and more fresh fruit and vegetables; no added salt (the role of sodium on blood pressure was discovered thirty years earlier). In an eminently quotable phrase, Hay opined, 'The diet should be such that the patient likes what he eats, though it is obvious that he should not be allowed to eat just what he likes'.

Anti-hypertensive drugs were deemed of secondary importance at the time; there were not many available and those that were occasionally used, such as mercury and thiocyanate, had serious adverse side effects. This contrasts with today, when in developed countries, up to 10–20 per cent of the population are taking drugs to lower their blood pressure. Some cases of hypertension can be traced to secondary consequences of an underlying pathology (e.g. kidney disease, diabetes). However, in about 90 per cent of cases there is no clear cause—this is known as 'essential' hypertension, although it is known from epidemiological studies that there is a strong correlation with age, family history, being of African or Caribbean origin, having a high salt diet, lack of exercise, obesity, smoking, and excessive alcohol intake.

The lack of an underlying pathological mechanism suggests that there are many different ways of damaging the body's physiology. One possible explanation is that a variety of genetic and environmental conditions lead to the same outcome—constriction of the arteries; this reduced volume leads to an increase in blood pressure in order to maintain the same rate of fluid flow. This is analogous to attaching a hosepipe to a water tap. Without touching the tap (flow rate) the pipe is squeezed. The narrowing of the jet of water increases the pressure and the smaller volume is ejected at a higher speed. However, the total volume flow of water in litres per minute will remain unchanged (after all you have not touched the tap). So forcing a smaller volume at a higher pressure and flow will maintain the same rate of blood flow (and hence oxygen and nutrient delivery) around the body.

Therefore people can live for many years with hypertension and suffer no apparent ill effects; oxygen can still readily be transported in the hypertensive individual. However, the hosepipe analogy illustrates the problem. You may get equally wet walking in front of a low-pressure or a high-pressure hosepipe; but only the latter can blow you over. Years of forcing blood around the body at a higher pressure can cause local damage to the tissue. Microscopic tears form in the artery walls; scar tissue attracts and accumulates biological 'debris', including dead cells (platelets and macrophages) and lipid crystals derived from cholesterol. These are called 'atherosclerotic plaques'. They can further restrict blood flow. Or even worse, burst. In the latter case a clot can form, causing a heart attack or stroke.

The dietary, lifestyle, and exercise regime advocated by doctors in the 1930s largely works by preventing plaque build-up and facilitating the biological availability of molecules that can dilate (open) arteries. However, this is not always enough to reverse hypertension. In the absence of effective drug therapy doctors occasionally resorted to an operation called a 'sympathectomy'. This removes nerves in the spinal column that are part of the sympathetic nervous system. Originally this involved the sawing of ribs to access the nervous tissue; this developed into an only slightly less damaging procedure in which the surgical incision was made above the collar bone. Nowadays, sympathectomy is still only used to treat certain disorders of an overactive sympathetic nervous system such as excessive sweating or Raynaud's disease. Even so, and using minimally invasive endoscopic techniques, it remains a controversial tool.

The sympathetic nervous system mediates, among other responses, the neuronal and hormonal 'flight and fight' response, leading to the release of adrenaline (termed 'epinephrine' in the USA) and a rise in blood pressure. The rise in blood pressure and flow is obviously useful as part of the stress response, for example to evade capture by a predator. However, could long-term perturbations of this system be a primary cause of clinical hypertension? This is an ongoing and topical debate. Even if an overactive sympathetic nervous system was not the cause of hypertension, dramatically decreasing its activity is a guaranteed method to decrease blood pressure and hence treat hypertension (hence the ill-advised sympathectomies practised in the 1940s and 1950s). Nowadays the drugs of choice to lower sympathetic activity are beta blockers. These are so called because the adrenaline released into the bloodstream elicits its effects on organs via binding to proteins on the surface of cells called 'beta-adrenergic receptors'; blocking these receptors with a drug prevents the actions of compounds like adrenaline and drops heart rate and blood pressure.

Beta blockers were discovered by the Scottish scientist James Black while working at ICI Pharmaceuticals; he then left to join Smith, Kline & French Laboratories, where he was instrumental in developing the histamine-2 blocking drugs used to treat stomach ulcers. Black's vision—building on Paul Ehrlich's 'magic bullet' strategy—was to look for proteins in the body that controlled key aspects of pathophysiology and then to design molecules that could interact with them. The award of the Nobel Prize in 1988 recognized Black's key role in rational drug design.

Beta blockers are now used routinely to treat both hypertension and, more especially, heart disease. Interestingly at the 1984 Los Angeles Olympics a medical exemption for the use of beta blockers was requested for entire shooting teams. Was there a correlation between the ability to shoot straight and severe heart and blood pressure problems? Maybe, though it is also possible that an attempt was being made to take advantage of a loophole in the anti-doping regulations. Beta blockers reduce hand tremor induced by anxiety and improve shooting accuracy in elite athletes. This loophole has now been firmly shut (and led to a North Korean athlete being stripped of two medals at the Beijing 2008 Olympics).

A variety of other drugs are also currently used to treat blood pressure. A low dose diuretic can be used to increase fluid loss. Both salt and water loss in the urine is enhanced. However, it is the loss of salt that is key. Excessive salt in the blood plasma attracts water from the tissue into the blood to decrease the salt concentration. This results in more fluid in the blood, increasing blood volume and hence pressure. Lowering the salt in the body fluids can reverse this effect.

If hypertension is persistent, patients are most likely to be treated with drugs that target specific pathways that the body uses to control blood pressure. For example angiotensin is a protein that can trigger secretion of the hormone aldosterone from the adrenal gland. In its active form angiotensin can directly constrict blood vessels, while aldosterone enhances salt and water retention, so raising blood volume. Both these effects increase blood pressure. Angiotensin is converted into its active form by an enzyme called 'Angiotensin Converting Enzyme' (ACE). An ACE inhibitor drug prevents this activity, keeping angiotensin in its inactive form; this will therefore drop the patient's blood pressure. The first angiotensin inhibitor was discovered in the venom of a South American pit viper by the Brazilian scientist Sérgio Ferreira. While this might be considered unusual at first glance, snake venom contains a cocktail of bioactive compounds that target the nervous and cardiovascular systems. In appropriate diluted forms, this can be the basis for new drugs. So the same ACE inhibitor designed to catastrophically drop a victim's blood pressure could, in lower doses, be used to help a patient's chronic hypertension. The only problem with using the snake venom ACE inhibitor clinically was that it was a small protein and easily digested in the gut. So nowadays patients are given artificially designed inhibitors that are orally active and can be taken in pill form, such as perindopril, captopril, enalapril, lisinopril, and ramipril.

The metal calcium controls many processes in the body. Its entry into muscle cells triggers muscle contraction. Preventing this entry can therefore reduce the force of contraction of the heart and the ability of arteries to constrict. Both of these will have the effect of decreasing blood pressure. Calcium enters muscle cells via specific protein-based channels. Drugs that block these channels (calcium channel blockers) are therefore highly effective at treating hypertension. Examples include verapamil, diltiazem, and nifedipine. Surprisingly, many of these drugs, when given in pill form, have far more potent effects if the patient has recently eaten a grapefruit or drunk grapefruit juice. This is because the drugs are partially broken down in the gut by an enzyme, a fact taken into account when determining the dosage. Grapefruit juice inhibits this drug-metabolizing enzyme; drinking this juice with the drug can therefore cause more of the drug to reach the patient, resulting in an overdose with potentially fatal consequences.

Blood flow

This chapter has focused on blood pressure, for the obvious reasons that it is both easy to measure and can inform on a variety of modern health problems. However in terms of biological function the actual pressure itself is not the relevant factor. The flow of blood is what delivers the oxygen and the nutrients to cells, and not the pressure. This point was made explicitly over eighty years ago by the Austrian pharmacologist Adolf Jarisch when he said:

> It is a source of regret that the measurement of flow is so much more difficult than the measurement of pressure. This has led to an undue interest in the blood pressure manometer. Most organs, however, require flow rather than pressure.

Bernoulli's work showed that blood pressure provided the force that produced blood flow. Arterial blood pressure does vary, becoming higher in the more peripheral vessels. Evolution has however resulted in different parts of the body responding differently to changes in pressure. The most dramatic example of this is autoregulation. This is the phenomenon by which blood flow to an organ is independent of changes in blood pressure. It was predicted as long ago as 1902 by the English physiologist William Bayliss who, in an eloquent passage in the *Journal of Physiology*, wrote:

> the peripheral powers of reaction possessed by the arteries is of such a nature as to provide so far as possible for the maintenance of a constant flow of blood through the tissues supplied by them, whatever may be the height of the blood pressure, except so far as they are directly overruled by impulses from the central nervous system.

Bayliss's suggestion was first demonstrated in the kidney in 1931, and in many more organs in the 1950s and 1960s.

A typical autoregulation curve for the brain is illustrated in Figure 20. At high blood pressures, a decrease in pressure causes the artery to contract, decreasing blood flow linearly. However, in the normal range (50–150 mm Hg), artery volume

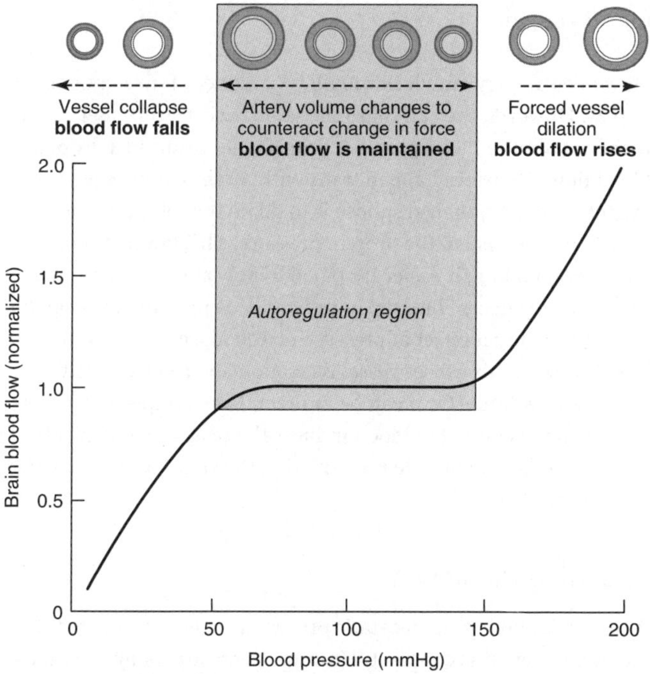

20. Autoregulation of blood flow in the brain. Effect of changing mean arterial blood pressure on brain blood flow. Shaded region represents the limits of blood flow autoregulation. Circles above the graph represent the cerebral arteries. Above the plateau region there is forced dilation as the intravascular pressure overcomes the maximal muscular tension, and below the plateau there is vessel collapse as the wall tension cannot compensate for falling intravascular pressure.

increases as pressure drops, counteracting the expected fall in flow; the protective effect of autoregulation ensures flow is insensitive to pressure in this range. However, below 50 mm Hg, autoregulation fails, and blood flow drops linearly with pressure with ultimately catastrophic consequences. As might be expected autoregulation is stronger, and maintained over a wider range of pressures, in organs that are critically dependent on a constant supply of oxygen, such as the brain, heart, and kidney, when compared to less oxygen-sensitive organs such as the skin or gut.

How does biology outwit Bernoulli? A number of mechanisms are in play. However, they all share the same basic feature. Bernoulli's theory predicts a blood pressure drop should result in a drop in blood flow. This does happen transiently, even in autoregulatory organs. However, their response is to dilate the relevant blood vessels in response to the drop in pressure. This lowers their resistance, making it easier for blood to flow and counteracting the pressure effect. The drop in resistance as pressure falls can be caused by a direct effect of pressure on the muscle walls of the blood vessels; this causes vessel relaxation and a consequent increase in volume. Or it can be indirect. For example, a decrease in oxygen tension in the blood induces the release of chemicals that then relax the muscle wall, dilating the vessel and enhancing blood flow.

Changing the flow

Autoregulation is a homeostatic process designed to ensure that blood flow remains constant. However, there are many occasions when an organism actively requires a change in blood flow. It is relatively easy to imagine what these are. In the short-term, blood supplies oxygen and nutrients. When these are used up rapidly, or their supply becomes limited, the response will be to increase blood flow. The most obvious example is the twenty-fold increase in oxygen and glucose consumption that occurs in skeletal muscle during exercise when compared to rest. If there were no accompanying increase in blood flow to the muscle the oxygen supply would soon run out. Less dramatically, but equally importantly, the brain diverts blood flow to where it is needed most—where there is the most neural activity. This ensures the healthy brain never runs out of oxygen. More subtle changes occur in other organs.

There are hundreds of molecules known that have the ability to increase or decrease blood flow; far too many to describe in detail in this chapter. However, one particular example stands out for historical, and current medical, interest. The surface of all blood vessels is lined by a thin layer of cells, the 'endothelium'. Endothelial cells form a barrier between the blood and the surrounding tissue, controlling access of materials into and out of the blood. For example white blood cells can enter or leave the circulation via interacting with the endothelium; this is the route by which neutrophils migrate from the blood to the site of tissue damage or bacterial/viral attack as part of the innate immune response. However, the endothelium is not just a selective barrier. It also plays an active role in blood physiology and biochemistry. In 1980 the US scientist Robert Furchgott discovered that the endothelium released a factor that 'relaxed' blood vessels; and then had the great sense to give it an acronym (EDRF)—Endothelium Derived Relaxing Factor—that made perfect sense as to its function (not always a feature of scientists' acronyms). Relaxation means that the muscles within the blood vessel wall stop contracting as forcefully. Partially released from this grip, the vessel expands and increases its volume. EDRF is therefore classed as a vasodilator (as opposed to a molecule that decreases blood vessel diameter which is termed a 'vasoconstrictor'). A vasodilator, such as EDRF, will thus increase the amount of blood reaching a tissue; in contrast, a vasoconstrictor will decrease blood flow. Blood flow is therefore tightly controlled by concentration changes in vasoconstrictors and vasodilators.

Furchgott's discovery was one of those great scientific moments that at first glance appear like serendipity. Of course in reality these random happenings occur all the time; it is the mark of a great scientist to recognize their significance. Furchgott worked in his lab with strips of artery prepared from the aorta of a rabbit. For about fifteen years he was getting variable results. About 35 per cent of the time he couldn't get his experiments to work at all, however hard he tried. He even joked that maybe his 'good' technicians made strips that worked and his 'bad' technicians made lousy ones that didn't. However, one day he thought he should test his idea. Maybe some technicians were overzealous in preparing the strips, accidentally rubbing the surface. This would remove the thin layer of endothelial cells. When Furchgott did this deliberately he was indeed able to show that the arteries could only be made to relax when they had an intact layer of endothelium. Hence the discovery of EDRF.

By the 1980s there were a number of molecules known that could affect blood flow. These were small organic carbon-based molecules, similar to those described earlier that can affect blood pressure (e.g. amphetamine, beta blockers). It came as a real shock, however, to see quite how small EDRF itself turned out to be. Not only was it the smallest ever signalling molecule discovered, but it was not even organic (containing no carbon). It also turned out to be neither solid nor liquid but a gas—and a gas, moreover, previously thought of as an environmental pollutant. The molecule in question was nitric oxide (NO, consisting of one atom of nitrogen bound to one atom of oxygen). The identification of nitric oxide as EDRF was discovered independently by Salvador Moncada in the UK and Louis Ignarro in the USA.

The haem iron in the oxygen-binding protein haemoglobin (see Chapter 3) reacts rapidly with nitric oxide. Indeed both Ignarro and Moncada showed that nitric oxide was likely to be EDRF as adding haemoglobin in the laboratory prevented its action. The same thing happens in the body. If a red blood cell bursts it releases its haemoglobin into the circulation, destroying nitric oxide. The destruction of a vasodilator causes vasoconstriction, tightening blood vessels, decreasing blood flow and increasing blood pressure.

Nitric oxide is destroyed by the haem in haemoglobin. However, it exerts its vasodilator effect by reacting with another haem protein called 'guanylate cyclase'. Unlike the case with haemogobin, nitric oxide binds to the haem iron in guanylate cyclase but is not destroyed by it. Instead the binding activates an enzyme function that increases the concentration of a molecule called 'cyclic GMP'. This molecule then induces the vasodilation, opening the blood vessels. In 1998 perhaps the world's most famous drug, Viagra, was shown to prevent erectile dysfunction by prolonging the lifetime of cyclic GMP in the penis, hence maintaining the requisite vasodilatory blood volume increase.

Glyceryl trinitrate (GTN) is a medicine that has been used for over one hundred years to treat angina and heart complaints. In 1977, Ferid Murad discovered that GTN worked by activating guanylate cyclase. Murad noted that nitric oxide had the same effect and postulated that GTN works by releasing nitric oxide, which activates guanylate cyclase. Glyceryl trinitrate is also commonly known as the explosive nitroglycerin (the medical name was changed so as to not scare patients). Nitroglycerin replaced gunpowder's reign as the industrial explosive of choice and ushered in the modern era of explosives, heralding a revolution in construction and, of course, warfare. The Swedish industrialist Alfred Nobel was responsible for the commercialization of nitroglycerin. Athough Nobel did not invent nitroglycerin itself, he discovered ways of using it safely by tempering its explosive power in the form of dynamite and gelignite. This made him a vast fortune and, ultimately, funded the scientific prizes that bore his name. Nobel himself suffered from angina and was treated with nitroglycerin, noting the irony that the molecule that had made his fortune for its destructive qualities was now being used therapeutically to treat him.

Given this history, the discovery of EDRF and the nitric oxide signalling pathway was clearly a Nobel Prize waiting to happen, and in 1998 the prize was duly awarded.

Chapter 6
Blood transfusion

Transfusing animal blood

In 1628, Harvey had shown that the blood circulated around the body. Even the harshest sceptics of his theories admitted defeat when Malpighi showed the existence of the capillaries that linked arteries and veins. Yet removing, not adding, blood was still the main medical procedure in the immediate centuries after Harvey. While this seems strange to our modern world-view, it made sense both practically and theoretically to the Renaissance mind. Practically, it is easy to remove blood, at least as long as you know how to close the wound. However, adding blood requires more skill. Left outside the body, blood readily forms an insoluble clot. Even before it clots, skill and specialized tools are required to deliver anything more than a few drops into a vein. And of course we know now that severe immune reactions can occur if the blood is from an animal or a human with a different major blood group.

Nevertheless, the suspicion remained that, if bloodletting worked by rebalancing bad blood humours, infusing fresh 'good' blood (or transfusing good blood for bad) could be of great benefit to a sick patient. Drinking blood was a source of power and energy for many mythical beasts, not just the vampires we are familiar with in today's culture. In the 15th and 16th centuries, a number of

Italian and German scientists explored these ideas. In 1489 the Italian philosopher Marsilio Ficino proposed that drinking the blood of healthy young men could rejuvenate the elderly or those with illnesses. Indeed it seems that an attempt was made to cure Pope Innocent VIII of his stroke by giving him the blood of three 10-year-old boys. More dramatically the Hungarian princess and serial killer, Countess Elizabeth of Bathory, was alleged to have drained all the blood from over 600 young girls to feed her restorative blood baths.

These stories may sound horrible to modern ears. However, these events all occurred before Harvey's time and before the discovery of oxygen. Removing arterial blood would have been dangerous as this contained the 'vital spirits'. However, a venous transfusion would likely be deemed safe as feeding the boys afterwards should swiftly restore nutritive blood into their veins. There may be less of a defence for the Countess. Yet we should remember that blood inspires myths. The Pope was (obviously) a prominent Catholic and the Countess a prominent Protestant. Many of the more lurid versions of these tales have the hand of the Reformation or Counter Reformation upon them. Blood baths were not mentioned at the Countess's trial and only appeared in print many years later. The trial may have had more prosaic underpinning. The King owed her family a lot of money and the all too convenient evidence against her at the trial of her servants was probably obtained under torture.

More serious claims to be the first to perform a blood transfusion were made by German and Italian scientists in the 17th century. The German chemist Libavius wrote a book in 1615 suggested connecting the artery of a donor to that of a recipient using silver tubes. The assumption was that the healthy spirit of the donor would revitalize that of the sick person. This would have been dangerous, as placing an arterial line in a patient is a skilled task even today; nor is it easy to see how such a direct transfer could have succeeded—if the blood pressure of the donor was significantly higher, some flow might have been initiated, but the pressures would soon equalize and the flow stall. The Italian physician Francesco Folli did claim to have performed a blood transfusion between two animals in 1654 in front of Grand Duke Ferdinand II. However, it is doubtful that this event happened as described. Folli waited until 1680 to write a book describing the transfusion, blaming the gap on the fact that his invention was so important it should only be shared with monarchs. A less charitable view is that he wanted to claim precedence over the scientists who had actually succeeded in performing transfusions in the period between 1654 and 1680.

Whether the idea originated in Germany or Italy, the practical success of blood transfusions was firmly rooted in a cross-Channel rivalry between English and French scientists. Scientists of today take for granted the cut-throat rivalry between researchers. Being the first to publish is key to both fame and future research grants. We should perhaps not be too harsh on ourselves. The problems confronting science frequently have a unique solution—there is only one answer, and getting it first is all. This contrasts with art; as Sir Peter Medawar famously said in his book *Advice to a Young Scientist*, 'the twenty years Wagner spent on composing the first three operas of *The Ring* were not clouded by the fear that someone else might nip in ahead of him with *Götterdämmerung*'.

Nevertheless, we still sometimes feel guilty about being so cut throat and precious about winning the scientific race. After all, for many of us, our vision of science is as a collective endeavour with the brightest and most altruistic minds working together for the good of mankind. It is therefore worthwhile to remember that the beginning of modern science featured just such a battle. The Royal Society, the first formal scientific society, was formed in London in 1662; four years later, in response, the Académie Royale des Sciences was founded in Paris. Both countries would later claim to be the first to suggest the idea of a formal organization of scientific scholars. Fights over priority were not just restricted to scientific experiments, but to the creation of organizations that managed the research itself.

It was scholars from these societies, and their immediate precursors, who joined battle over claims to be the first to have performed a successful blood transfusion. A friend of Harvey's from his Oxford days, Francis Potter, attempted to transfuse blood between hens in his Somerset parsonage in 1652, but with little success. His attempt was doomed to failure on two fronts. First, he was unaware of how to control the clotting phenomenon and, when blood was removed from the body, the clot all too quickly prevented a subsequent transfusion; secondly, the small surface veins he could access in the hen had little driving pressure and collapsed.

Back at Oxford, attempts were made to inject solutions of various chemicals into blood. The new ideas of Harvey indicated that it no longer mattered where an infusion was made—the circulatory system would carry the medicine around the whole body. The first successful test in 1656 involved using a quill to infuse opium (dissolved in red wine) into the large vein in the hind leg of a dog. The narcotic effect was almost immediate. Further studies quickly followed using emetics and laxatives, with results far more immediate than if these compounds were given by mouth. Attempts were made to provide nutrition by infusion, including broth, milk whey, and even beer. In 1657 a human subject ('an inferior domestic who deserved to be hanged') was used; extract of crocus was the infusion, but the man passed out and the study was rapidly stopped.

The scientists involved in these studies were no minor luminaries. John Wilkins was married to the sister of Oliver Cromwell, then Lord Protector of England; Robert Boyle would become one of the founders of modern chemistry, his eponymous law describing the relationship between the absolute pressure and volume of a gas; and Christopher Wren would find a post-scientific career as an architect, most famously designing St Paul's Cathedral in London.

The journal of the Royal Society notes several attempts in 1665 to transfer blood between animals, both pigeons and dogs. Success was finally achieved by Richard Lower in 1666. He managed to directly connect the carotid artery of one dog into the jugular vein of another; the higher pressure in the artery and the direct blood connection between the animals overcame the problems Potter had with his hen studies. Lower's success was reported to the Royal Society in July and took pride of place in the December issue of the journal *Philosophical Transactions*.

Things were also heating up on the other side of the Channel. Between January and March 1667, several attempts were made in Paris to transfuse blood between two dogs by a team headed by Claude Perrault. Initially trying to connect leg arteries and veins, they finally succeeded using the neck method of Lower. However, this success was limited. In many cases the donor dog died from blood loss as too much arterial blood was removed; the recipient fared little better, probably due to a combination of blood clots and an adverse immune reaction. Weighing the animals before and after revealed that only two ounces had been transferred, corresponding to 60 ml of blood (for comparison a unit of whole blood transfused today contains 400–500 ml).

At this point enthusiasm in France diminished. In fact the final report on these studies concluded that infusion was unlikely to succeed. Reference was even made to the Greek myth of Medea, the wife of Jason (of Jason and the Argonauts fame). Medea magically rejuvenated her sick father-in-law, Æson, by first making a cut in the old man's neck to remove his blood. He was then rejuvenated with a magical potion, in part made from the old blood. However, the myths differ on how the sorcerer administered the potion, whether by getting Æson to drink it or by mixing it into his wounds. The French academicians quoted

Medea favourably to suggest oral transfusion was likely to be the best route. It is intriguing that even forty years after Harvey's discoveries of the closed circulatory system, the idea of blood being administered orally still held a strong sway on medical opinion.

Enter Jean-Baptiste Denis. Denis was a young man looking for a discovery to make his mark in French scientific society. Like Christopher Wren, he was a polymath. Following a Bachelor's degree in theology, he qualified in medicine, before obtaining a doctorate in mathematics. By the age of 27 he was a professor of mathematics and astronomy in Paris. Medical research was his hobby, but he soon realized that it could also become his claim to fame. Like Perrault's team, Denis had also been transfusing dogs in March 1667 and published his work in the French *Journal des Sçavans* the same month.

Denis followed this with the successful transfusion of blood from a calf to a dog; the study was designed to note the effects of mixing the 'necessarily' stronger blood of a large animal into that of a smaller, weaker one. Again note the view that the blood itself contained the essence of the animal. A larger animal must require stronger blood. It was not enough to have a larger heart to pump it around the body, the material itself was assumed to be different. We are steeped in the modern idea of a blood transfusion merely as a means to increase blood volume and oxygen delivery. Yet we should not be too quick to dismiss the idea of blood as a rejuvenating agent. Parabiosis is a technique for physically connecting two organisms—in effect creating artificial Siamese 'twins'. In the 1970s it was shown that joining the blood circulation of an old rat to a younger rat significantly extended the lifespan of the older rat. More recent studies have also shown parabiosis is able to reverse brain degeneration in animal models.

Denis knew that the fame would come from being the first to cure a sick human by transfusing the blood of a strong healthy animal.

His opportunity came when a teenage boy presented with complications arising from a fever. Like George Washington this boy had been excessively 'treated' with bloodletting; in this case twenty times over a two-month period. The fever had remained, but was now accompanied by listlessness and extreme fatigue. Denis took the radical view that it was lack of blood that was the problem, not too much blood. What little that remained could not boil off the fever, nor could it carry sustenance and power to the tissues. He proposed to treat this problem with the addition of fresh vigorous animal blood. He chose a sheep for this purpose, directly connecting a tube from its carotid artery to a tube in a vein in the young boy's arm. Driven by the higher pressure in the artery, the blood flowed into the boy. The boy recovered well and Denis considered the transfusion a great success, though, with modern hindsight, it is more likely that this was due to the cessation of the bloodletting therapy than to the addition of the small amount of sheep blood that was transfused.

Denis went on to transfuse a healthy man, who suffered no ill effects. He was then persuaded to attempt a transfusion of a dying man, Baron Bond. The Baron died shortly after the transfusion, but Denis—probably correctly—assigned this to the effects of severe gangrene compounded by excessive bloodletting. To really show the benefits of transfusion, Denis needed a patient with a stronger body. In December 1667 he therefore attempted the transfusion of blood from a healthy calf into an insane man, Antoine Mauroy, the idea being that the infusion of new healthy humours would restore sanity to his charge (Figure 21). Suffice to say that he had three transfusions. The first two seemed initially to have positive effects, but these did not last. Viewed from today's perspective, the symptoms are consistent with a severe immune reaction to the foreign blood; Mauroy died shortly after his third transfusion. Denis was put on trial for murder. At the trial, his defence team accused Mauroy's wife of the act. Denis was acquitted, but the judge ordered that any further transfusions would need to be approved by the Parisian faculty of medicine.

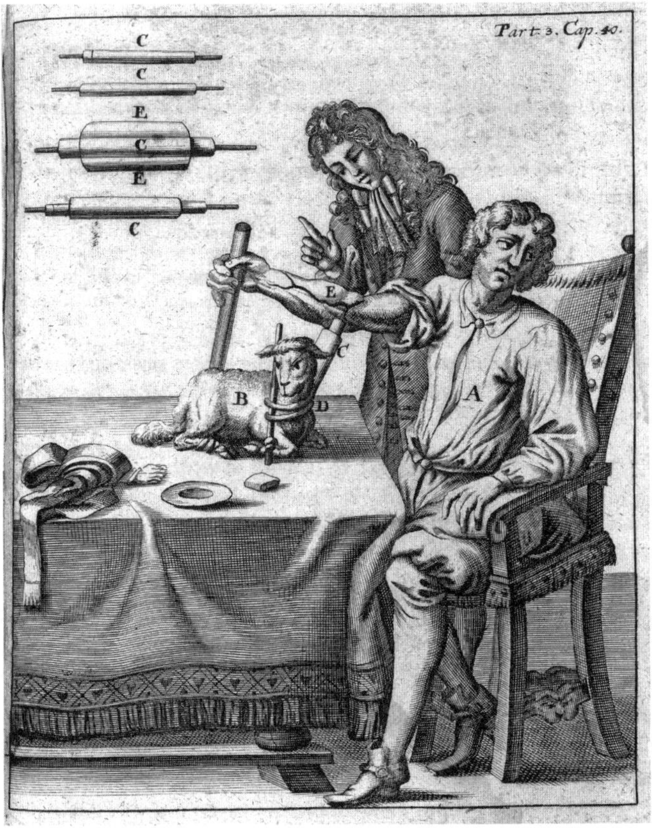

21. A picture of the first blood transfusion by Denis.

Meanwhile, the English had been driven into action by Denis's animal–human transfusions. Like Denis, Lower wanted to transfuse blood from an animal into a healthy man with some mental disturbance, hopefully changing the person's character for the better. Lower performed two transfusions from a lamb into a 'slightly mad' young Cambridge graduate called Arthur Coga.

Lower used a similar method to Denis. He calculated the amount he transfused by bleeding the lamb's blood into a bowl for the same amount of time that Coga was transfused. This suggested the transfusion was of 9 ounces of blood (250 ml, or about half a modern blood unit). However, the length of the piping between the lamb and Coga, and a decreased blood flow rate, probably means this was a significant overestimate. Lower's two transfusions had underwhelming results; the patient seemed unharmed, but there was no obvious benefit. Lower wanted to continue this work but he was overtaken by the Denis trial and the subsequent controversy. The French medical authorities never approved another animal-to-human transfusion. In 1675 the Pope passed an order banning blood transfusion. Protestant countries also acted, the English parliament banning the technique in 1678.

Given the ultimate failure of the technique, the Anglo-French fight over claiming scientific precedence abated. But it was bitter at the time. Denis submitted his paper to the prestigious English journal—*Philosophical Transactions*—in July 1667. This showed he was the first to perform an animal-to-human blood transfusion (true) and also claimed credit for being the first to think of the idea of such a transfusion ten years earlier (questionable). However, the journal issue was later re-published with Denis's claims watered down and precedence for the original idea given to the English. Denis cried foul; surely the English blood transfusionists had seen his article and persuaded the journal publisher to rewrite the article? In fact in this instance Albion was not being perfidious. The publisher of the journal, Henry Oldenburg, had originally intended to edit Denis's piece prior to publication, moderating the claims and noting the English precedents from Wren to Lower. But Oldenburg was suddenly arrested and imprisoned in the Tower of London on charges of 'dangerous designs and practices' (essentially acting as a spy). On his subsequent release from prison he was horrified that Denis's article had been published without any editing at all. It was for this reason that he recalled the original journal issue and published an alternative, less French-friendly, article in a revised issue.

With the benefit of hindsight, we can see the claims of Oldenburg and Denis were both inflated. The idea of intravenous blood transfusions originated with German (Libavius) and Italian (Folli) scientists; Englishmen (Wren, Lower) were the first to infuse fluids into humans and the first to perform animal-to-animal blood transfusions; and the French (Denis) were the first to transfuse animal blood into a human. If this narrative occurred today it would have been heralded as a triumph for European science. Except of course that although the operation was a success, the patient died—literally, in the case of Denis's transfusion.

Transfusing human blood

One hundred and fifty years passed. With transfusions in seemingly permanent disrepute, doctors carried on happily bleeding their patients. However, it became increasingly evident to some that the complete ban on human blood transfusion, even as a last resort, was too severe. John Leacock, a Barbadian-born doctor working in Edinburgh, revisited experimenting with animal-to-animal transfusion. Crucially he showed how important it was to transfuse within species; his attempt to transfuse a cat with canine blood was spectacularly unsuccessful. In his one publication on transfusion in 1817 Leacock made a strong case for transfusion, stating that

> when the danger is imminent, and the common means are ineffectual, as when a parturient women trembles on the brink of the grave from uterine haemorrhage, or when a soldier is at the point of death from loss of blood, what reason can be alleged for not having recourse to this last hope?

His words inspired James Blundell, an obstetrician working in Edinburgh at the same time. Blundell was concerned with the amount of blood lost from his patients during birth (his precise words were stronger: Blundell was 'appalled at my own helplessness at combating fatal haemorrhage during delivery'). Then, as now in many developing countries, post-partum haemorrhage was the major cause of maternal death.

In fact Blundell's first attempt at a human-to-human blood transfusion was not for one of his obstetric patients. On 22 December 1818, he transfused a patient with stomach cancer who suffered from 'obstinate vomiting'. The patient died two days later. Between 1818 and 1829, Blundell undertook ten transfusions. Over half of the patients died, though some were probably very close to death (or actually dead) prior to the transfusion. However, a few survived and some prospered, including, in 1829, one woman given 150 ml of blood following severe post-partum haemorrhage (again the volume is much lower than we might expect to have a significant effect today). Blundell was not present at the birth itself but brought in only when other stimulants—port and brandy—had failed to have any marked benefit. Following her three-hour transfusion, 'she felt as *life* were infused into her body'. It is interesting that the language of transfusion had by then changed significantly from that of a misbalance of the humours. Blundell's patients viewed blood itself as life-giving. Following an almost 2,000-year, Galen-inspired hiatus, the scientific view now coincided with the mythos. Blood was a life-giving, not a humour-altering, fluid.

Blundell's method was essentially the same as that of Denis, connecting an artery in the forearm of the donor directly to the vein of the recipient. He later experimented with safer methods using veins from both donor and recipient. In this case the blood was removed from the donor's vein and injected into the recipient's. However, you had to work fast; anything more than a few seconds outside the body would result in irreversible clotting.

Yet despite all these precautions, some of Blundell's patients suffered from fevers and passed dark urine. Although he did not know it at the time, this was a result of damaged haem being expelled from the body following an autoimmune response to a donor with an unsuitable blood type. However, he famously refused to revert to the use of animal blood, stating,

> What is to be done in an emergency? A dog might come when you whistled, but the animal is small; a calf might have appeared fitter for the purpose, but then it had not been taught to walk properly up the stairs!

In Blundell's time, women in Scotland gave birth at home and presumably, given this quotation, upstairs. The beauty of working in obstetrics was that a willing donor was easy to find. In the famous 1829 case, Blundell arrived to find three male midwives attending to the mother. He used one, a Mr Davies, as the blood donor. Other transfusionists of the time made use of the father's blood.

Blundell's success, however limited, encouraged others, especially in continental Europe, to experiment with transfusion. The results were very mixed and the practice did not gain widespread approval. Two major issues remained at the end of the 19th century: the problem of clotting, which all were aware of; and the problem of blood group incompatibility, which no one had the slightest idea even existed.

In North America these problems led to the use of another fluid that appears to modern views to be a backward step: milk. Milk infusion was part of Sir Christopher Wren's 17th-century nutrition studies. But nutritive support was not the goal at this time. The view was that milk globules could transform into white cells and then into red cells. In one sense this appears too literal to be scientific—milk is white, white blood cells are white. However, this is less strange if viewed in a modern light. White blood cells were of unknown function and present in much smaller quantity than red cells, just what you might expect for a transient population on the road to being transformed into mature red cells. A cell of exactly this type exists in blood. Although most red blood cells are made from haemopoetic stem cells in the bone marrow, blood does contain a small population of immature red cells, reticulocytes, still in the final stage of the maturation process. The infusion of milk therefore has an interesting resonance with current attempts to infuse artificially grown reticulocytes as an alternative to standard red cell transfusions.

Be that as it may, milk does not grow into red blood cells, and infusion of cow and goat's milk came with even worse side effects than the blood transfusions they were trying to replace. Two facts doomed milk in the late 1880s. The last refuge of the milk enthusiasts was to use human milk, but this was shown to be no better than cow milk. At the same time, infusions of saline (salt) solutions were developed and became increasingly popular. Saline solutions are still the first line of defence today following trauma; although they cannot transport oxygen, they do increase the volume of blood fluid, albeit transiently. But at the turn of the 20th century they had the even more considerable advantage of not having the adverse side effects associated with blood or milk.

For blood transfusions to ever make a recovery the key issues of blood clotting and adverse side effects needed to be resolved. In 1875 the Swedish biochemist Olof Hammarsten showed that adding calcium accelerated the rate of blood clotting (we now know the mechanism for this is that key enzymes in blood platelets that catalyse fibrin formation require calcium for their function). It therefore made sense to use chemicals that bind calcium to try to prevent clotting. Calcium ions are positively charged; adding negatively charged ions such as oxalate and citrate neutralized the calcium, preventing its clot-promoting action. Studies in animal blood at the turn of the 20th century proved promising. So in 1914 the Belgian Albert Hustin and the

Argentinian Luis Agote used sodium citrate in human blood transfusions. The precise citrate levels are crucial; binding in the recipient's blood can directly cause toxicity in itself as adequate blood calcium is crucial for muscle and nerve function. It was left to an American, Richard Lewisohn, to determine the precise dose of citrate that worked as an anticoagulant, without poisoning the blood. The use of citrate enabled donor blood to be stored. Removing the donor from the vicinity of the patient paved the way for today's blood banks, which use essentially the same dose of citrate.

At the same time as anticoagulants were being discovered, the reason why some blood transfusions failed even when there were no clots was becoming clear. It had been shown that animal blood given to humans tended to clump together or agglutinate, eventually bursting and releasing free haemoglobin and causing kidney damage. In the early 1900s, working in Vienna, Karl Landsteiner showed the same effect could occur with human-to-human transfusion. The trick was the ability to separate blood cells from serum. This enabled mixing blood cells from a variety of donors with plasma from a variety of participants. Using his laboratory staff as subjects, Landsteiner showed that only some combinations caused the agglutination reaction. Some donor cells (now known as type O) never clumped. Others clumped depending on the nature of the plasma in a reproducible manner. A careful study of Landsteiner's results revealed the ABO blood type distinctions described in detail in Chapter 2. Versions of these agglutination tests still form the basis of checking transfused blood today. Except in the most dire emergency (when type O is given) samples of the blood in the donated blood bag are always tested against the recipient's plasma prior to any transfusion.

Allowing for the blood type removed many of the adverse reactions in human-to-human transfusion that had previously been attributed to factors such as introducing air bubbles into the recipient's blood circulation. Safe modern blood transfusion had arrived.

Blood banks

The idea of setting up large fixed storage centres for blood was developed in the Soviet Union in the 1930s by Serge Yudin and Alexander Bogdanov. The word 'blood bank' itself was first used by Bernard Fantus for the first US facility at Chicago's Cook County Hospital. But bringing it to the masses required organization and industry. The catalyst for this was war. Soldiers need blood and they need it on the battlefield, or at the very least in nearby mobile hospitals far away from home.

Enter two unlikely heroes—Norman Bethune and Charles Drew. Bethune was a Canadian surgeon who, after visiting the Soviet Union in 1935, campaigned in favour of a state medical care system. He joined the Communist Party in 1936. Soon after the outbreak of the Spanish Civil War, like many socialists and communists of the time, he gave up his job and volunteered for the Republican cause. Once there, he saw the reality of the German bombing of Madrid, the wounded lying on the streets bleeding to death. Spanish doctors such as Frederico Duran-Jorda had set up a large static blood bank in other cities such as Barcelona. But Bethune wanted to get his blood out to where it was needed. With Canadian colleagues he set up his own blood transfusion service, collecting blood from 1,200 donors in the first day. He wanted to defeat fascism, not just save civilians on the streets of Madrid. He took his donated blood to the frontline in refrigerated vans. 'The wounded were dying searching for blood. Now the blood can move. Now blood can search out the wounded. It's the same as organising a milk route.' The mobile, almost guerrilla medicine suited Bethune's rebellious character (Figure 22). Unable to conform to the *diktats* of the more organized republican armies that emerged in 1937, he left Spain, eventually ending up in China setting up

22. Norman Bethune (right) and his mobile Canadian Blood Transfusion Unit during the Spanish Civil War.

mobile hospitals for Mao Tse-tung's Eighth Army fighting behind enemy lines against the Japanese. Cutting himself during one of his thousands of operations, Bethune died from blood poisoning in 1939. Bethune became a communist hero in China. During the Cultural Revolution, Mao wrote a one-page epitaph which became compulsory reading in all Chinese schools.

The outbreak of the bombing blitz against Britain in 1940 also required more mobile forms of blood. Charles Drew, a distinguished Harvard surgeon, managed the 'Blood for Britain' programme. Drew developed separation and dehydration methods to safely collect and ship over 5,000 litres of dehydrated blood plasma from the USA to Britain. Although plasma is not used for emergency transfusion nowadays, Drew's blood separation methods are still broadly the same as used today. Ironically, given that Drew was the first African-American to be awarded a PhD from New York's prestigious Columbia University, the samples bound for Britain were segregated so that only Caucasian blood was sent. Later in the war, the US Red Cross did accept African-American blood, but still insisted on labelling the bags separately from white blood, a custom that persisted until 1950. The science of racial equivalence was not debated, but the Red Cross feared that take-up of the programme would suffer without segregation. It was accepted by the 20th-century public that blood or plasma donation—especially if given in war—was a short-term life-saving treatment, rather than a cure for mental illness or bad humour. But the popular idea that blood contained someone's genetic essence and could 'contaminate' a transfusion recipient had clearly not yet gone away.

Nowadays there is general acceptance, except among some religious communities, that transfused blood is a product that functions in a purely physical way to replace lost oxygen-carrying-capacity function in the recipient. However, even if appropriately typed for the major blood groups, a transfusion of blood products could still cause unwanted side effects. The most extreme was well-known to Drew—that of contamination with bacteria. Indeed, before Drew's more careful sterile techniques, the British recipients labelled plasma as 'liquid death'. Therefore a modern blood transfusion centre is like a well-run factory (Figure 23). Donated blood is classified and converted into healthcare products by separation techniques such as centrifugation. Whole blood can be separated into packed red cells, plasma, and platelets. All these have their distinct uses. The cells are typed and barcoded for transfusion; plasma is sold for patient use either directly or as a source of useful biological products such as albumin and immunoglobulins; platelets are given to patients, such as cancer sufferers undergoing chemotherapy, in whom production of the body's own platelets in the bone marrow is depressed and circulating levels are low or poorly functional.

23. A modern blood factory. The NHS Blood and Transplant centre in Filton (near Bristol, England) is the world's largest manufacturing, testing, and distributing centre. It produces 830,000 units of red cells a year and tests 1.2 million donor samples. Filton distributes blood products to more than 130 hospitals.

When transfusions go wrong

No blood product can be made completely sterile, no matter how carefully it is processed. The best that can be done is to ensure that no new bacteria or viruses are added during the purification, storage, and transportation processes. Nothing can be done to inactivate any viruses that are already present in the donor's blood, for the harsh treatments necessary to do this would inevitably damage the viability of the product or be prohibitively expensive to implement on the industrial scale that the blood market has become. Worse still, new blood-borne viruses are constantly emerging; it is these that have been the main threat to the blood transfusion services that emerged worldwide after the end of World War II. These concerns were epitomized by the rise of HIV/AIDS in the 1980s. In one sense this was a triumph of blood science. A new infectious disease was recognized and, in a reasonably short space of time, the virus was identified. An antibody-screening test was developed soon after. Policies were put in place to limit the viral presence in donor blood; any contaminated blood passing through this social screening of inappropriate donors could still be caught by the antibody test and the blood discarded. Blood products such as clotting factors for haemophiliacs were heat-treated to destroy the HIV virus.

These triumphs were the precursors to the rapid response to the discovery of new viruses in today's blood transfusion market. The success was, however, overshadowed by an international scandal that resulted in many unnecessary deaths and the imprisonment of many of the scientists and administrators deemed responsible. Mistakes were indeed made. In the USA there was an overreliance on recruiting paid blood from donor populations (such as prisoners or homeless people) who were more likely to be suffering from infectious diseases such as hepatitis and HIV. The US has a mixed market in blood, the Red Cross competing with commercial providers. For commercial reasons some agencies only used the HIV tests on their new blood, leaving older contaminated products on the shelf. In France, there was a delay in using validated HIV tests developed by US companies until a rival French product had been developed. Japan continued to use unsafe imported American products when it knew them to be contaminated. Haemophiliacs suffered most as they needed multiple doses of clotting factors, which come from multiple donors. In the 1980s over half the US haemophiliac population was HIV positive.

In the 1980s and 1990s the realization of the scale of these blood scandals led to civil and criminal cases in many countries including France, Denmark, Germany, Italy, Japan, Canada, and the US. In Britain, justice proceeded at a more leisurely pace. Between 1970 and 1991, tens of thousands of people were infected with hepatitis C and/or HIV through blood products supplied by the National Health Service. However, the only public inquiry into this affair, the Penrose Inquiry, finished in 2015, and was restricted to exploring the situation in Scotland alone.

Viral contamination of blood and blood products has not been the only blow to the transfusion industry. With the increasing societal calls for evidence-based medicine, the whole idea of blood transfusions has come under scrutiny. Recent studies of past blood transfusions given to patients in a hospital setting have revealed worrying findings. Patients given red blood cells during a surgical operation or in critical care were shown to have *worse* outcomes than those where less, or no, blood was used. Blood stored in blood banks for longer times (closer to its 35–42 day limit) seemed particularly likely to trigger these adverse responses. The mechanisms for the worse outcome are unknown but are assumed to be due to undesirable effects on the immune system; transfusion both enhances inflammation and suppresses immunity.

Statistical analysis of historical data is never as good a clinical guide as well-designed, randomized clinical trials. These are difficult to do for blood. Unlike a new pharmaceutical product or surgical technique, it is not ethically possible to do a simple randomized clinical trial of a blood transfusion versus a saline alternative. Blood is already considered to be a life-saving product and it would therefore be unethical to randomize patients to a placebo group. However, two recent (2015) clinical trials have looked at the age of blood storage. One, called 'ABLE', looked at the age of blood cells donated to critically ill adults; the other, called 'RECESS', looked at the effect of red cell storage duration on patients undergoing cardiac surgery. Both studies found no differences between very fresh (< 8 days storage) and averagely aged blood. However, for ethical reasons they were not allowed to randomize a patient group to receive only the oldest blood (> 30 days) for which there is the greatest safety concern. Still, for now, transfusion services around the world have breathed a collective sigh of relief; they are not about to be forced to shorten the shelf life of their red cells, which could have had catastrophic effects on their supplies.

Transfusions have the potential to save lives by increasing blood volume, raising blood pressure, and enhancing oxygen delivery. They are a vital treatment for acute trauma and surgery. In conditions of chronic blood loss, the body can sometimes be tricked into making more of its own blood cells by treatment with hormones such as erythropoietin. However, in extreme cases of anaemia nothing works as well as a red blood cell transfusion.

Blood transfusions work, but it is impossible to completely remove the risk of adverse immune reactions, not to mention the ever-present threat of new viruses. The blood clotting proteins that haemophiliacs need to survive are now made artificially by genetic engineering techniques, with no chance of infection. Could the same be done for blood cells? Is artificial blood the future?

Chapter 7
Epilogue: the future of blood

The nature of our blood can vary over the course of our life. For example our blood type can change following illnesses such as infections, and certain cancers that alter the sugar chains on the surface of the red cell. However, the most dramatic change occurs following a bone marrow transplant. The recipient—usually suffering from blood cell tumours such as leukaemia or lymphoma—is treated with chemotherapy to destroy their own faulty bone marrow cells. They are then injected with haematopoietic stem cells harvested from a compatible donor. These are the precursors of all new blood cells (Figure 3). This requires a bone marrow donor who is very closely matched immunologically, frequently a close relative such as a parent or sibling. Except in the unlikely event that the donor is an identical twin, the recipient will eventually start making blood cells that are identical to those of the donor, which can include being of a different blood group type. The recipient's blood has been permanently transformed by modern medicine in a way that would have been beyond the wildest dreams of the early transfusionists seeking to change a person's personality via altering their blood humours.

We now know that the genetic nature of your blood has a very limited effect on your general health. Except in cases of dire clinical need, modern medicine has no wish to give someone a blood transplant. As we learnt in the last chapter, blood transfusion is a treatment to alleviate the lack of oxygen delivery and low blood pressure caused by anaemia—due to chronic disease, surgery, or trauma. However, we also noted the potential pitfalls of transfusions. Red blood cells need refrigeration, only last for a limited shelf time, need to be matched to the donor carefully, and—most crucially—cannot be made virus-free. It has long been a dream for synthetic biologists to manufacture an artificial blood substitute that could be stored and transported easily, didn't require blood typing, was long lasting, and could be guaranteed to be pathogen-free. This dream has been well-funded both by governments and industry. The military have also invested heavily. For while the modern versions of Bethune's mobile blood banks are very sophisticated, they are only feasible when soldiers are based in defined—and readily defended—areas. So while in the Iraq war, US soldiers mostly patrolled minutes away from a blood bank, this was not the case in conflicts such as those occurring in the mountains of Afghanistan.

Three fundamentally different ways have been attempted to replace red blood cell transfusions. The first uses a completely chemical approach and makes use of perfluorocarbons, inert chemicals that, in liquid form, can dissolve gases without reacting with them. They came to prominence in World War II when as part of the Manhattan Project they were used to chemically insulate highly reactive uranium intermediates when developing the atomic bomb. Having said that, the most famous example is the Teflon used to coat non-stick frying pans.

Perfluorocarbons can dissolve oxygen much more effectively than water. In a famous example Leland Clarke showed in 1966 that a mouse immersed in an oxygen-saturated perfluorocarbon solution was able to breathe 'underwater'. The problem with their use as a blood substitute is that the amount of oxygen dissolved in these solutions is linear with increasing pressure. This means that the solution lacks the advantages of the sigmoidal binding curve of haemoglobin, which has evolved to maximize the amount of oxygen captured from the limited fraction found in air (20 per cent oxygen). However, to deliver the same amount of oxygen as haemoglobin, patients using the less efficient perfluorocarbons in their blood need to breathe gas that is almost 100 per cent pure oxygen (Figure 24); this restricts the use of these compounds. Nevertheless one such compound (Fluosol) was briefly licensed for use in the US, and another (Pertforan) in Russia and Mexico. However, practical difficulties in product administration, coupled with adverse immune reactions to the foreign particles, have resulted in these products falling out of favour.

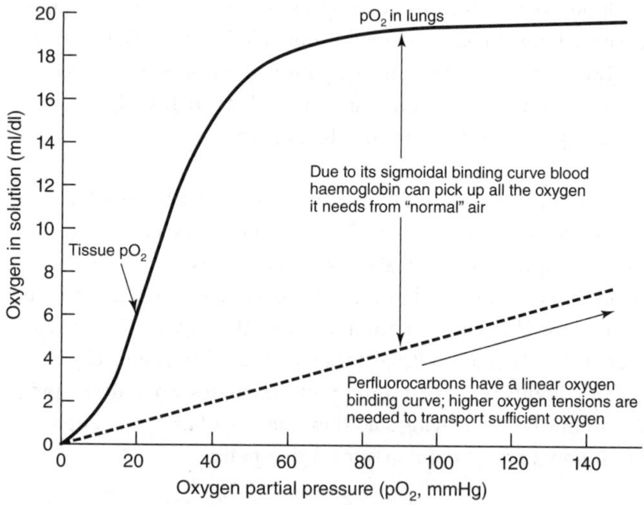

24. How artificial chemical blood substitutes deliver oxygen. Biology versus physics: the biologically evolved haemoglobin binding curve means that blood can pick up the maximum amount of oxygen when we breathe 'normal' air (21 per cent oxygen). The physics of oxygen binding in a perfluorocarbon solution means that a higher oxygen tension is required in the lungs to achieve the same effect; this is usually achieved by breathing gas mixtures containing a much higher percentage of oxygen.

The second type of blood substitute makes use of haemoglobin biology. Initial attempts used purified human haemoglobin itself. Although this had the potential to carry oxygen, it suffered from the drawback that mammalian haemoglobin has not evolved to function outside the confines of the red cell. The four-subunit tetramers are continuously breaking down into two-subunit dimers and re-forming. Inside the cell this is not a problem. However, outside the dimer is small enough to be filtered through the kidney. Therefore extracellular haemoglobin is continually lost through the kidney and passed out in the urine. The solution was to copy the organisms, such as earthworms, that have evolved to transport oxygen outside a red cell. These giant haemoglobins (erythrocruorins) are held together by strong covalent bonds. Although one company (*Hemarina*) is directly attempting to exploit these giant haemoglobins as extracellular oxygen carriers, others have used alternative methods to mimic this stability in mammalian haemoglobin (Figure 25). These include: synthesizing new intramolecular bonds to cross-link protein subunits within a tetramer; forming intermolecular bonds to cross-link between tetramers; and coating the surface of the tetramer with polyethylene glycol (PEG). Attempts have even been made to encapsulating the tetramer inside an artificial cell.

Despite almost a billion dollars of research and development there is no haemoglobin-based blood substitute in general use today (although one product, Hemopure, is currently still licensed for human use in Russia and South Africa, and its veterinary equivalent was approved in the USA and Europe). The problem for the lack of uptake is not that blood substitutes cannot replace red blood cell function. A variety of products have been shown to stay in the vasculature for several days, provide volume support, and deliver oxygen. However, they have suffered due to adverse side effects, most notably cardiac complications. It is not completely clear why this should be so, but it is likely to be due to issues arising from the reactivity of haemoglobin outside the secure environment of the red cell (Figure 26). The reactive iron

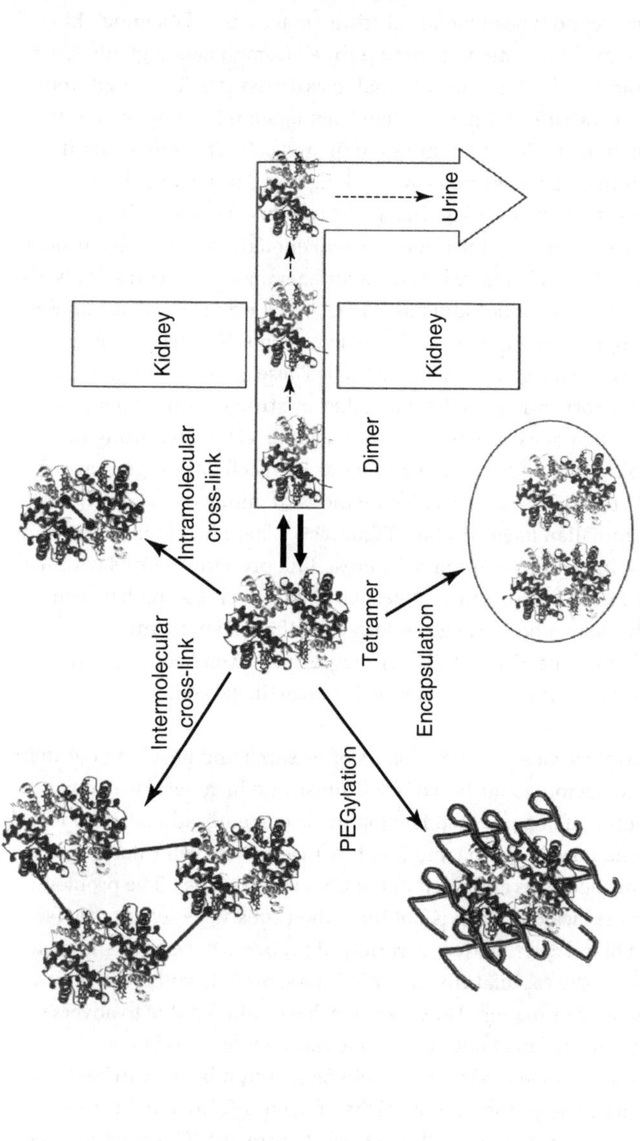

25. Keeping a blood substitute in circulation.

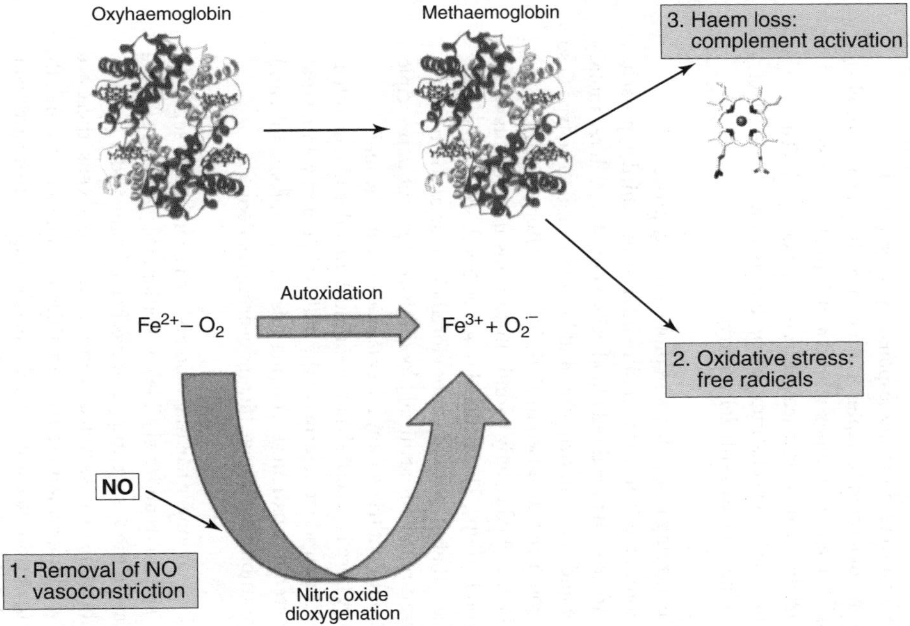

26. Toxicity of extracellular haemoglobin. **(1) Reaction with the vasodilator nitric oxide (NO) to form methaemoglobin (nitric oxide dioxygenation). (2) Spontaneous oxidization (autoxidation) to form methaemoglobin and superoxide radicals. (3) Haem falls out of methaemoglobin.**

can scavenge nitric oxide and thus remove a key molecule that controls blood flow (Chapter 5); it can directly create reactive oxygen-free radicals, of the kind that white cells use to destroy invading pathogens (Chapter 2); and if the haem falls out it can trigger an adverse immune response by triggering the complement system (Chapter 3). In nature the plasma proteins haptoglobin and haemopexin bind and detoxify any free haemoglobin and haem released from red blood cells. The challenge for blood substitute research is to mimic these effects in a product that can still deliver oxygen.

Despite ongoing research, these problems may prove to be insurmountable. There is therefore interest in a third approach. This is to grow artificial red blood cells using stem cell technology. These could be made virus-free and be engineered to be type O so that it could be transfused to all recipients. Alternatively they could be matched exactly to difficult-to-transfuse patients with rare blood groups. The artificial blood cells still would have the drawback that they could not be stored for years at room temperature like the artificial blood substitutes; but in principle they should not trigger any adverse side effects. The main difficulty here is practical, not theoretical. Blood is like no other biomedical product in terms of the bulk weight and volume that is delivered to a patient. Producing this safely, reproducibly, and in large amounts is a huge bioengineering challenge.

Even if we no longer feel that blood is at the core of our self and soul, it still holds an irresistible fascination; this is as true for the scientists of the 21st century as it has been for the wider public throughout history. As well as synthetic red blood cells, there are teams working on ways to create artificial platelets to staunch the bleeding of trauma patients, and others trying to create artificial killer white blood cells or synthetic blood vessels. But nature yields its secrets slowly. TV dramas and films may show artificial blood as a reality for vampires. For humans, there is still some way to go.

References

Chapter 1: A history of blood

Anger and seeing red

Fetterman, A. K., Robinson, M. D., Gordon, R. D., and Elliot, A. J. (2011) Anger as seeing red: perceptual sources of evidence. *Social psychological and personality science* **2**, 311–16.

The discovery of capillaries

Pearce, J. M. (2007) Malpighi and the discovery of capillaries. *European neurology* **58**, 253–5.

Chapter 2: What is blood?

'Blood is a juice of rarest quality'

Goethe, J. W. von (1889) *Faust*. Translated by Bayard Taylor, publisher Ward, Lock and Co., London.

Blood group antigens

Lin, Y., Pavenski, K., Saidenberg, E., and Branch, D. R. (2009) Blood group antigens and normal red blood cell physiology: a Canadian blood services research and development symposium. *Transfusion medicine reviews* **23**, 292–309.

Snake venoms

Kini, R. M. (2006) Anticoagulant proteins from snake venoms: structure, function and mechanism. *Biochemical journal* **397**, 377–87.

Chapter 3: Fighting disease

The history of vaccination

Riedel, S. (2005) Edward Jenner and the history of smallpox and vaccination. *Proceedings (Baylor University Medical Center)* **18**, 21–5.

Agostino Bassi

Porter, J. R. (1973) Agostino Bassi bicentennial (1773–1973). *Bacteriological reviews* **37**, 284–8.

Paul Ehrlich

Turk, J. L. (1994) Paul Ehrlich—the dawn of immunology. *Journal of the Royal Society of Medicine* **87**, 314–15.

Elie Metchnikoff

Tan, S. Y., and Dee, M. K. (2009) Elie Metchnikoff (1845–1916): discoverer of phagocytosis. *Singapore medical journal* **50**, 456–7.

Chapter 4: Haemoglobin

Haemoglobin structure and function

Brunori, M. (2014) Variations on the theme: allosteric control in hemoglobin. *The FEBS journal* **281**, 633–43.

The varied biological functions of haemoglobin

Giardina, B., Messana, I., Scatena, R., and Castagnola, M. (1995) The multiple functions of hemoglobin. *Critical reviews in biochemistry and molecular biology* **30**, 165–96.

Haemoglobin in birds that fly at high altitude

Scott, G. R. (2011) Elevated performance: the unique physiology of birds that fly at high altitudes. *The journal of experimental biology* **214**, 2455–62.

Haemoglobin and the woolly mammoth

Campbell, K. L., Roberts, J. E., Watson, L. N., Stetefeld, J., Sloan, A. M., Signore, A. V., Howatt, J. W., Tame, J. R., Rohland, N., Shen, T. J., Austin, J. J., Hofreiter, M., Ho, C., Weber, R. E., and Cooper, A. (2010) Substitutions in woolly mammoth hemoglobin confer biochemical properties adaptive for cold tolerance. *Nature genetics* **42**, 536–40.

Chapter 5: Blood pressure and blood flow

Early concerns about high blood pressure

Hay, J. (1931) A British Medical Association Lecture on 'The significance of a raised blood pressure'. *British medical journal* **2**, 43–7.

Adolf Jarisch quotation about blood flow and blood pressure

Jarisch, A. (1928) Kreisslauffragen. *Deutsche Medizinische Wochenschrift* **54**, 1213.

Autoregulation of blood flow

Bayliss, W. M. (1902) On the local reaction of the arterial wall to changes of internal pressure. *Journal of physiology (London)* **28**, 220–31.

Johnson, P. C. (1986) Autoregulation of blood flow. *Circulation research* **59**, 483–95.

Chapter 6: Blood transfusion

Parabiosis

Villeda, S. A., Plambeck, K. E., Middeldorp, J., Castellano, J. M., Mosher, K. I., Luo, J., Smith, L. K., Bieri, G., Lin, K., Berdnik, D., Wabl, R., Udeochu, J., Wheatley, E. G., Zou, B., Simmons, D. A., Xie, X. S., Longo, F. M., and Wyss-Coray, T. (2014) Young blood reverses age-related impairments in cognitive function and synaptic plasticity in mice. *Nature medicine* **20**, 659–63.

First report of human-to-human blood transfusion

Blundell, J. (1829) Successful case of transfusion. *Lancet* **I**, 431.

Scandals relating to tainted blood transfusions

Feldman, E. A. and Bayer, R. (eds.) (1999) *Blood feuds: AIDS, blood, and the politics of medical disaster*. Oxford University Press, Oxford.

Department of Health Policy paper (2011) Estimate of total number of hepatitis C-infected individuals in UK infected over the period 1970–1991. In *Review of the support available to individuals infected with hepatitis C and/or HIV by NHS-supplied blood transfusions or blood products and their dependants* pp. 41–2.

Age of stored blood cells for transfusion

Lacroix, J., Hebert, P. C., Fergusson, D. A., Tinmouth, A., Cook, D. J., Marshall, J. C., Clayton, L., McIntyre, L., Callum, J., Turgeon, A. F., Blajchman, M. A., Walsh, T. S., Stanworth, S. J., Campbell, H., Capellier, G., Tiberghien, P., Bardiaux, L., van de Watering, L., van der Meer, N. J., Sabri, E., and Vo, D. (2015) Age of transfused blood in critically ill adults. *The New England journal of medicine* **372**, 1410–18.

Steiner, M. E., Ness, P. M., Assmann, S. F., Triulzi, D. J., Sloan, S. R., Delaney, M., Granger, S., Bennett-Guerrero, E., Blajchman, M. A., Scavo, V., Carson, J. L., Levy, J. H., Whitman, G., D'Andrea, P., Pulkrabek, S., Ortel, T. L., Bornikova, L., Raife, T., Puca, K. E., Kaufman, R. M., Nuttall, G. A., Young, P. P., Youssef, S., Engelman, R., Greilich, P. E., Miles, R., Josephson, C. D., Bracey, A., Cooke, R., McCullough, J., Hunsaker, R., Uhl, L., McFarland, J. G., Park, Y., Cushing, M. M., Klodell, C. T., Karanam, R., Roberts, P. R., Dyke, C., Hod, E. A., and Stowell, C. P. (2015) Effects of red-cell storage duration on patients undergoing cardiac surgery. *The New England journal of medicine* **372**, 1419–29.

Chapter 7: Epilogue: the future of blood

Design and function of red blood cell substitutes

Modery-Pawlowski, C. L., Tian, L. L., Pan, V., and Sen Gupta, A. (2013) Synthetic approaches to RBC mimicry and oxygen carrier systems. *Biomacromolecules* **14**, 939–48.

Alayash, A. I. (2014) Blood substitutes: why haven't we been more successful? *Trends in biotechnology* **32**, 177–85.

Further reading

Chapter 1: A history of blood

Gregory, A. (2001) *Harvey's heart: the discovery of blood circulation.* Icon Books Ltd, Duxford, UK.

A book that places Harvey's work in its historical and cultural context, without sacrificing a clear explanation of its scientific underpinning.

Meyer, M. L. (2005) *Thicker than water: the origins of blood as symbol and ritual.* Routledge, New York.

This is the definitive book on blood as a cultural metaphor. It is written for an academic, rather than a general, audience, but still contains great stories. It covers a much wider range of societies than I was able to fit into this book.

Hayes, B. (2006) *Five quarts: a personal and natural history of blood.* Random House, New York.

A very accessible history written by a non-scientist. It expertly and movingly intermingles a history of blood with the personal joys and struggles of living with an HIV positive partner.

Chapter 2: What is blood?

Bain, B. J. (2004) *A beginner's guide to blood cells*, 2nd edn. Blackwell, Oxford.

A short, simple book that covers the basic facts clearly and comprehensibly. Although written for trainee biomedical scientists it is easily understandable by the non-specialist. It has the advantage of containing many colour illustrations of normal and abnormal blood cells.

Chapter 3: Fighting disease

Sampayrac, L. (2012) *How the immune system works*, 4th edn, Wiley-Blackwell, Oxford.

This is a rarity—a book that explains the complexities of the immune system step-by-step to the novice. It includes some very clear diagrams. Although it assumes a very basic knowledge of biology, the author claims it is 'a short book that tells, in simple language, how the immune system fits together, without the jargon and the details'. And it is.

Chapter 4: Haemoglobin

Terwilliger, N. T. (1998) Functional adaptations of oxygen-transport proteins. *Journal of experimental biology* **201**, 1085–98.

A not too technical overview of the wide variety of different haemoglobin-like molecules found in nature.

Schechter, A. N. (2008) Hemoglobin research and the origins of molecular medicine. *Blood* **112**, 3927–38. Freely downloadable at: <www.bloodjournal.org/content/112/10/3927.full-text.pdf>

A short overview of haemoglobin structure, function, and diseases by someone with many years' experience of the field.

Chapter 5: Blood pressure and blood flow

Booth, J. (1977) A short history of blood pressure measurement. *Proceedings of the Royal Society of Medicine* **70**, 793–9. Freely downloadable at: <http://www.ncbi.nlm.nih.gov/pmc/articles/PMC1543468/>

A well-written overview with interesting historical photographs of devices used from the 18th to 20th centuries.

Marsh, N. and Marsh A. (2000) A short history of nitroglycerine and nitric oxide in pharmacology and physiology. *Clinical and experimental pharmacology and physiology* **27**, 313–19.

A brief overview of the fascinating story of these molecules and the people who discovered them. An explosive story of gases, prizes, and drugs.

Chapter 6: Blood transfusion

Starr, D. (1998) *Blood: an epic history of medicine and commerce.* Alfred A. Knopf, New York.

A history of the science and business of blood transfusion ending with the 1990 scandal of HIV-tainted blood.
Moore, P. (2003) *Blood and justice*. John Wiley and Sons Ltd, Chichester, UK.
A dramatic interpretation of the events surrounding the first human blood transfusion in 17th century Paris that is both readable and informative.
Overfield, J., Dawson, M., and Hamer, D. (2008) *Transfusion science*, 2nd edn. Scion Publishing Ltd, Bloxham, UK.
A comprehensive overview of all aspects of transfusion.

Chapter 7: Epilogue: the future of blood

Silverman, T. A. and Weiskopf, R. B. (2009) Hemoglobin-based oxygen carriers: current status and future directions. *Anesthesiology* **11**, 946–63. Freely downloadable at: <http://anesthesiology.pubs.asahq.org/article.aspx?articleid=1932745>
A report of a US FDA meeting that discussed the future of blood substitutes. It comprises an interesting combination of views from physicians, scientists, industrialists, and potential end users such as the US army and navy. The meeting came immediately after a controversial and highly critical review of the safety of the products, and became quite heated at times.

Index

A

B

C

D

E

I

J

K

L

M

N

W

X

Y

Online Catalogue

A Very Short Introduction

Our online catalogue is designed to make it easy to find your ideal Very Short Introduction. View the entire collection by subject area, watch author videos, read sample chapters, and download reading guides.

http://global.oup.com/uk/academic/general/vsi_list/

HUMAN ANATOMY

A Very Short Introduction

Leslie Klenerman

A vast subject that includes a strange vocabulary and an apparent mass of facts, human anatomy can at first appear confusing and off-putting. But the basic construction of the human body—the skeleton, the organs of the chest and abdomen, the nervous system, the head and neck with its sensory systems and anatomy for breathing and swallowing—is vital for anyone studying medicine, biology, and health studies. In this *Very Short Introduction* Leslie Klenerman provides a clear, concise, and accessible introduction to the structure, function, and main systems of the human body, including a number of clear and simple illustrations to explain the key areas.

www.oup.com/vsi